Praise for *Corpse Care*

"Our culture and economy have encouraged and perpetuated many unnatural separations and the handing over of nearly everything to experts. *Corpse Care* is a gift. The book teaches a history few of us know and allows us to reclaim our own death and the deaths of those we love. In so doing, it draws together the relationship between birth and death—that to die is to give life. This is the practice of resurrection."

—Mary Berry, executive director, The Berry Center,
New Castle, KY

"What is the revelatory potential of the corpse? Sanders and Parsons boldly confront us with the neglected question of an incarnational theology, and they address it with deep pastoral wisdom and critical historical awareness. Ironically, while Jews and Muslims find ready answers to that question in their own traditions, most Christians have forgotten even how to ask. This book belongs on the teaching agenda for every church."

—Ellen F. Davis, Duke Divinity School

"Sanders and Parsons provide a provocative exploration into practices related to our care for dead bodies. Well-researched and informed by diverse literature, their work notes the complicated history of care for corpses. Going beyond individualism, they name larger political, social, ecological, and theological implications for the way we deal with the dead. The conversations they invite forth are important for every pastor, seminarian, congregation, and community."

—Joretta Marshall, Brite Divinity School,
Texas Christian University

"From Sophocles's *Antigone* to the green burials of today, Cody J. Sanders and Mikeal C. Parsons provide a stunning and comprehensive description of how human beings tend to the dead. They reveal the wisdom and the humanity at stake in how all of us travel the journey from humus to human to humus once more. This book is a treasure!"

—Thomas G. Long, author of *Accompany Them with Singing: The Christian Funeral*

"*Corpse Care* is a deep dive into the history and present practices of how we relate to and treat the physical remains of humans. It is fascinating how culture, philosophy, and theology have shaped these practices and how the practices can also affect our relationship with the natural world. The book shows that seeing the corpse as a part of the web of life can help end our destructive assault on that web. I read most of it in one sitting. While I have read death studies for decades, I still found this book revelatory and intensely interesting."

—Billy Campbell, MD, co-founder and co-director of the first green cemetery in the United States, Ramsey Creek Preserve, Westminister, SC

"There is a deep fissure in our fundamental death-to-earth connection, brought about by relinquishing care of our dead and embracing practices that separate us from natural processes. This rich account provides a much-needed depth of perspective on how and why healing that disconnect can and should occur. Sanders and Parsons deepen the critical environmental and theological discourse over what to do with our bodies after death as an act toward climate resiliency and spiritual reconciliation by exploring what got us here and what will, hopefully, lead us home."

—Lee Webster, natural burial and funeral reform advocate; author, educator, and end-of-life and after-death educational nonprofit leader

Corpse Care

CORPSE CARE

Ethics for Tending the Dead

Cody J. Sanders
Mikeal C. Parsons

Fortress Press
Minneapolis

CORPSE CARE
Ethics for Tending the Dead

Cover design: Kristin Miller
Cover image: Female Corpse by Hyman Bloom; The Jewish Museum, New York / Art Resource, NY

Print ISBN: 978-1-5064-7131-0
eBook ISBN: 978-1-5064-7132-7

In loving memory of
Charles Maddox (1929–2020)
and
Barbara Hornik (1933–2020)

Contents

Preface

This book joins a growing corpus of literature devoted to the history of deathcare and its contemporary practices. This literature approaches issues surrounding the corpse from a variety of perspectives: sociological, ecological, legal, and so on. What is often missing in these other works, and what we hope to contribute through this study, is a sustained theological reflection on the place of the corpse in the larger web of life. As we will argue throughout the book, what is done with our corpses is a theological concern with implications for how we see ourselves as human beings within a context of belongingness to the rest of the planet. Even those studies that explicitly deal with the "body" from theological perspectives either ignore the corpse or, worse, dismiss the dead body as an inappropriate subject for theology proper. With *Corpse Care: Ethics for Tending the Dead*, we intend to redress this deficiency. The corpse is revelatory in so many ways.

The project began in a coffee shop in Cambridge, Massachusetts, in April 2017. During a research leave at Harvard Divinity School, Mikeal Parsons had been a participant in the congregational life of the Old Cambridge Baptist Church (OCBC), where Cody Sanders serves as pastor. This project was one Cody had been thinking about and working on for a long time while teaching courses on death and dying in several institutions of theological education, including Andover Newton Theological School and Chicago Theological Seminary, as well as part of his ongoing pastoral care at OCBC. His description of that work and plans for a volume on practical theology and corpse care piqued Mikeal's interest, who saw intersections with his own work on perceptions of bodies in early Christianity and its larger Greco-Roman environs.

That conversation led to an application for a Louisville Institute (LI) collaborative inquiry grant. We recruited June Hobbs, an English professor at Gardner-Webb University and an expert in cemetery markers (and coauthor of *Tales and Tombstones of Sunset Cemetery*, McFarland Press, 2021). We also enlisted the collaboration of Rochelle Martin, a registered nurse with specialty certification in psychiatric and mental health nursing who also educates and advocates for community-based, environmentally conscious after-death home funeral care through her initiatives "Funeral Alternatives" and "One Washcloth." The research question we proposed to explore was, *How can constructive practical theological approaches to the corpse and practices related to its care and disposition inform the evolution of deathcare praxis in North American religious communities and specifically among Christian congregations?*

With LI funding, the team embarked on several field research excursions. In the summer of 2018, we traveled to Conyers, Georgia, to visit Honey Creek Woodlands at the Monastery of the Holy Spirit—a religiously owned conservation burial ground. We interviewed Joe Whitaker, the founding director of Honey Creek. We also visited Wendy Eidson, director of Phoenix Funeral Services, one of the few female undertakers in a male-dominated profession, who has facilitated over 1,400 natural burials. On the same trip, we visited Ramsey Creek Preserve in Westminster, South Carolina, the first conservation-level natural burial preserve in the United States, and spoke with its founder, Dr. Billy Campbell, and his spouse, Kimberley. We also visited several historic cemeteries, such as Oakland and South-View in Atlanta.

In the summer of 2019, Meg L. Winslow, Mount Auburn's curator of historical collections and archives, and Rabbi Joshua Segal, of the Association for Gravestone Studies, led the team on a tour of Mount Auburn Cemetery in Cambridge, Massachusetts, the first rural/garden cemetery in the United States. With monument expert Laurel Gabel, we toured King's Chapel Burying Ground, founded in 1630 and the oldest burying place in Boston proper, along with several other colonial-period burying grounds. We also assembled focus groups of clergy and laity representing communities of racial, ethnic, and denominational difference, whom we asked to engage the team's practical theological approach to the questions of corpse care and to provide feedback to the team on the central questions of the research.

We presented preliminary findings regarding contemporary corpse care at several professional conferences, both as a group and individually. The pandemic hit during the middle of the research and fundamentally changed the focus and shape of the project. Still, the core of the vision for the project persisted, and Cody has remained the driving force from beginning to end. In addition to the above-mentioned collaborators and interlocutors, we are grateful to the Louisville Institute for providing the funds for the needed field work and for extending the project time frame when interrupted by Covid-19. We are especially grateful also to June Hobbs and Rochelle Martin for their insights into and energy for the project. Baylor University provided the institutional support necessary for administering the LI grant. OCBC provided, and the Lily Endowment National Clergy Renewal Program funded, a sabbatical leave for Cody that coincided with the writing of the manuscript. Cody also wishes to thank Ashley Cozine, 2016–17 president of the National Funeral Directors Association (NFDA), for arranging for Cody to attend the NFDA International Convention and Expo in 2017. Mikeal's graduate assistants, Josiah Hall and Kyle Rouse, proofed the chapters and constructed the bibliography. Carey Newman of Fortress Press provided encouragement and expert advice for developing a better book.

Finally, Mikeal is grateful for his family and colleagues who listened with a healthy mixture of interest and patience to his incessant talk of death and corpses. Cody is grateful to his partner, Cody VanWinkle, for his surprisingly enthusiastic interest in corpse care; to his students at Andover Newton and Chicago Theological Seminary, whose interests and insights over the years have energetically fueled the project; and to Lee Webster for her continued interest in and support for the project.

A word about the cover of this book, beautifully designed by Fortress Press: The painting is by Hyman Bloom (1913–2009), a Latvian-born Jewish painter who lived most of his life in Boston, Massachusetts, and began engaging the corpse as a major subject of his art in the 1940s. Cody serendipitously encountered Bloom's work at an exhibit at the Museum of Fine Arts in Boston in 2019. We are grateful that his is the image you first encounter when picking up this text. We hope that what Bloom saw in the corpse as a subject of art, we can convey in treating the corpse as a theological subject: simultaneously material and mystical, a site of pain and beauty, inviting a relationship of both absence and presence with the dead, and an object worthy of sustained attention for the living.

A significant aspect of tending the dead is remembering them. Cody and Mikeal dedicate this volume to the memory of Cody's grandfather, Charles Maddox, and Mikeal's mother-in-law, Barbara Hornik, who both died in April 2020. *Requiescant in pace.*

Cody J. Sanders, Old Cambridge Baptist Church
Mikeal C. Parsons, Baylor University

Introduction

ONE DAY WE will all become dead bodies.

When the Spanish waged imperialist war against the people of Mexico in the early sixteenth century, in addition to death by the sword, the colonizers also brought death by disease. Smallpox ravaged the people of Mexico such that it disrupted the funerary rituals of cremation and ritual burial of the ashes because there were simply too many corpses to care for in the customary way. In some instances, houses had to be simply brought down atop the corpses contained within.[1]

Additionally, many violent encounters between the European colonizers and the Indigenous peoples of North America included a disruption of deathways[2] as a means of violence. For example, the Mexica at times engaged in cutting open and offering body parts of the Spaniards as sacrifices, which aggrieved and offended the Spanish notion of the sanctity of the corpse informed by their Catholicism.[3] Similarly, the English colonizers demolished Powhatan temples in which the bones of their ancestors were buried as a method of uprooting them from land that held a deep significance for a number of reasons, not the least of which was that it was where the remains of their dead were interred.[4]

In the aftermath of Civil War battles, when thousands of corpses lay across the battlefield, the task of deathcare was overwhelming and nearly impossible. Drew Faust notes that survivors would often "shovel corpses into pits as they would dispose of animals . . . dehumanizing both the living and the dead through their disregard."[5] The Civil War disrupted the deathways of nineteenth-century America and stretched the government, the military, and nearly every community in the United States beyond its funerary capacity, indelibly changing the shape of deathcare in the ensuing century.

War is always attended by the necessity of caring for the dead whose corpses rest beyond the parameters of the time period's "good death." The United States spends $100 million every year trying to find and identify the eighty-eight thousand missing in action from every war since World War I.[6] We might remember in our own recent history the lengths to which government agencies went in order to recover and identify the remains of the dead buried under the rubble of the World Trade Center's Twin Towers when they fell on September 11, 2001.

While we recover bodily remains from mass graves created by wars or terrorist attacks, we dig them for the victims of plagues and pandemics. In the 1918 Spanish flu pandemic, corpses lined the streets of some neighborhoods in the United States, and few living persons remained to bury them.[7] Mass graves were dug. Wood to construct coffins ran out. In the aftermath of this pandemic, there were few public displays of mourning, and the rituals and ceremonies that traditionally accompanied the dead were absent.[8]

While the dead body was used as a weapon of war between Indigenous people and colonizers, the weaponization of the corpse has continued throughout US history. Between 1882 and 1942, over four thousand African Americans were lynched in the United States.[9] After the murder of African Americans at the hands of white people, the Black bodies-now-dead were desecrated. Body parts became "souvenirs," sliced from the corpse and distributed to the crowd. The United States Postal Service even made photographs of Black bodies left hanging in trees into postcards, mailed around the country.[10] The Black corpse itself was unwillingly enlisted as a signifier of racialized violence in Jim Crow America.[11]

Achille Mbembe painfully reflects on massacres like these that happen the world over and the ways in which "bodies stripped of being" are quickly returned to bones: "The most striking thing is the tension between the petrification of bone and their strange coldness, on the one hand, and the obstinacy in wanting to signify something at all costs, on the other."[12] The same might be said of the corpse itself—before it returns to cold bone: it signifies something to us about our treatment of bodies, both dead and alive, and activates movements toward justice in the wake of violence and death.

In addition to the corpses of the massacred becoming an obstinate signifier of injustice and, in prior eras, becoming weapons of war, the willing corpse has also been enlisted as an actor in nonviolent protest. In his art and writings in the midst of the US AIDS epidemic in the 1980s and '90s, activist artist David Wojnarowicz engaged with the corpse, exploiting "productively the hypervisibility of the person with AIDS in the discourse of American politics and mass media . . . and refashioned this vilified corpse into a political weapon to be detonated at the door of those directly responsible for perpetuating the epidemic."[13]

The activist group ACT UP (AIDS Coalition to Unleash Power) staged "die-ins" in conspicuous places like the lawn of the United States Food and Drug Administration and in the aisles of New York's Saint Patrick's Cathedral to bring attention to those dying of AIDS while the government and the church did nothing to help, instead disparaging gay people who were experiencing the brunt of the epidemic. But beyond people living with AIDS and their allies *posing* as dead, activists also turned to the AIDS corpse itself as an ally in activism. Funerals were politicized, with coffins put on public display and the cremains of friends brashly placed at sites of "perpetual wrongdoings" as a witness against the suffering wrought by the virus.[14] On October 11, 1992, the cremated remains of several bodies were even scattered on the lawn of the White House in an act of protest against the Bush administration's neglect of the AIDS crisis. In some circumstances, it becomes "difficult to distinguish the funeral from the demonstration."[15]

Our care *for* and *about* dead bodies in these instances is telling. We have a visceral reaction to any act we perceive as desecrating the corpse—whether it is dead soldiers whose corpses are lost on the foreign battlefield, or Michael Brown's body lying on the hot asphalt of Ferguson, Missouri, for four hours. We express shock at the sight of bodies buried without ceremony or the necessity of interment in the mass graves of a pandemic. We look back on lynching and are appalled not just by the wanton murder of Black people but also by the blatant indignity added by the racialized mutilation of their bodies after death. We develop the ability to weaponize the corpse against enemies in war, as well as the ability to enlist the corpses of dead comrades in acts of civil disobedience and protest. We regularly draw on the corpse's ability to *do* something and not just *be* something.

One day, then, we will all be dead bodies. This is distinct from saying that one day we'll all be dead. We have myriad cultural and religious impressions about what being dead will be like for us, from a resplendent heavenly existence, to an earthly reincarnation, to a deep and dreamless sleep. What is different about saying that one day we will all become *dead bodies* is that it stops us just short of those theological, spiritual, philosophical images of what comes *after* death, if anything. It confronts us with the materiality and meaning of our dead body and the significance of our own body *becoming* dead.

It is not just a morbid philosophical exercise in confronting our own mortality. Saying that we will one day *be* a dead body is a statement about our lives as embodied creatures, *incarnate* beings. Our fleshy incarnation holds within it the inevitability of death as part of its very substance. Our bodies contain within them, at this very moment, a sure unfolding toward death. Death is not, however, the *end* of our incarnation. Rather than an ending, death is integral to the process of our bodily *becoming*.[16] There is an element of desire to this becoming. Our incarnate bodies hold a desirous beingness-toward-death.

Importantly, we will still continue to *be* bodies—just dead ones rather than living ones.

What we do in relation to this stage of bodily becoming, the inevitability of our incarnation into death, presents us with a number of theological questions. But these are questions to which very few Christian theologians, ministers, or faith communities have given any careful attention in the last century. What we do in relation to our dead bodies is a subject that we do not often discuss in a theological way in our circle of friends, with our family, or within our congregations.

What we want "done" with our bodies after death is often reduced to a check mark on a funeral director's planning form under the heading "disposition."

Cremation or burial?
Embalming or no embalming?
No viewing, family viewing, or public viewing?

This casket or that urn?
Chapel service or graveside?

We've made the options for body disposition easy. Once the box is checked and the papers signed and the payment rendered, we no longer have to think about it. When we become dead bodies, our disposition is decided and paid for. We stop asking questions about the dead body.

Our bodies, however, do not make their dispositions quite so transparent to us. In addition to what we want to be *done* with something—how it is to be placed or arranged in space—"disposition" can also mean the qualities or natures or inclinations that something or someone possesses: a child with a cheery disposition, a dog with a disposition to run away when let off leash, or an employee with a disposition toward perfectionism.

One is a question of administrative disposition over the dead body, the other a question about the meaning of a body's disposition in the process of becoming dead: "the way our embodied nature yearns to unfold."[17] When we come to the administrative question of the *disposition* of a dead body in the first sense, the theological question becomes one of disposition in the second sense: In our beingness-toward-death, what do our embodied "natures" and our fleshy desires and our incarnate becoming suggest to us about what we should *do* with and in relation to our dead bodies?

Every embodied experience we have leading to the moment of our death suggests something about our incarnate body's desires—from our first memories of seeking shelter in the warmth of a parent's embrace, to our romantic impulses leading to a first kiss, to our body's draw toward the familiar grounded feeling of plunging our hands into the dirt of our gardens, or a sense of being lured into the woods to trek among the trees.

Bodies also have desires in relation to their becomingness-toward-death, a disposition of fleshy resistance against the simplicity of checkboxes on a form in the face of the body's deathly incarnation. Engaging theologically in our body's "disposition" raises critical questions about how we've come to relate to our bodies when they become dead.

Why have these choices of "disposition" and no others become the selections we are routinely given to make in relation to our dead body?

Where did these options come from, and what is their history?

How are contemporary options for body disposition related to grander narratives that attempt to make sense of our body's relationship to the wider world?

What is the meaning of these options to us when we face our own incarnate movement toward becoming dead bodies?

How do we conceive of our place among the community within the living web of life that is affected by the decisions we make in relation to our dead bodies?

Importantly, if the choices we are presently given for the *administrative disposition* of our dead bodies have a developmental history tacitly resting just behind each one of these options, are there also potential *futures* of deathcare toward which we might move if we turned a theological eye toward the question of *the body's disposition toward death*?

The Corpse as (a) Practical Theological Matter

Dead bodies matter to us. Whether or not we spend much time thinking about their meaning, the fact that they do *matter* is incontrovertible.

We are often given to trite and superficial statements about the disposition of our corpse in the presence of our family and friends:

> "Don't make a big fuss, just dispose of my remains."
> "Take me out with the trash. My body won't matter anymore."
> "I don't want anyone crying over my casket. I won't be there."

These statements have a history going all the way back to fourth-century BCE philosopher Diogenes the Cynic, who, according to Cicero, "ordered himself to be thrown anywhere without being buried."[18]

As glib as we, or our loved ones, or ancient philosophers might become from time to time about the supposed inconsequential nature of our dead bodies, we rarely act upon those glib musings. In fact, these statements are so discordant with our contemporary funerary practices that the incongruity between *expressed sentiment* and *actual practice* should alert us to important questions we have not yet learned to discuss. After all, the median cost in 2019 for a funeral with viewing and a conventional burial within a vault totaled $9,135.[19] It doesn't sound like our glib dismissal of the significance of the corpse has had an effect on our willingness to pay significantly for its final disposition.[20]

Any of our embodied practices that are tied this significantly to large sums of money of necessity become ethical questions—and thus, for religious communities, *theological* questions. But the economics of the corpse are not the only ways that the dead body matters *theologically.*[21] There are pastoral concerns as well. For example, how the community of faith gathers around one of its dead, speaking words and enacting rituals in the face of death.[22] Though we are often just as shallow in our abilities to act pastorally toward the corpse as we are in our skills at thinking theologically about the significance of the corpse.

Yet our dead bodies are *theological matter*—materiality imbued with meaning and deep significance related to questions of ultimate concern. And what we do with and in relation to our dead body is a *practical theological matter*, calling for critical thought in (re)formulating our practices of care.[23]

Family, friends, and ministers spend hours by the bedside of the dying in solicitous concern for their comfort, cultivating relational bonds to the end. Communities surround the bereaved family after the death of one dear to them, bringing food and flowers, offering words of comfort and expressions of companionship. But at the moment the body-deeply-loved dies, we routinely withdraw from the body-now-dead. We turn it over to the "professionals" to deal with. We converse about cherished memories and about missing feelings toward the dead. Clergy begin preparations for a funeral service where the dead body may or may not show up.

But what is being done with and in relation to *the dead body itself*—arguably the central character in the sacred drama of deathcare? We rarely have any real notion or ask any serious questions about the meaning that a body-now-dead holds for us as communities of faith speaking words and enacting rituals in the face of death.

Yet dead bodies can matter theologically in rich and instructive ways if we create the discursive space to hold questions about their materiality and meaning and about the significance of our own bodies *becoming* dead.[24]

What is the revelatory potential of the *corpse*?

How can the dead body teach us something vital about what it means to be human?

What mirror is held up to us when we look carefully and critically at how we relate to dead bodies, our own and others?

How can our interactions with the corpse illuminate our interactions with the larger living and dying web of life in which we are entangled in the tapestry of divine incarnation?

The corpse rests before us a limit-experience. Beyond this deathly embodiment, we can go no further in the flesh. Without the limit-experience of death, there would be no use for "God."[25]

If death and the dead body both stand as limit-experiences, inviting our theological inquiry and our spiritual praxis into the depths of mystery, we lose the significance of this experience if we forfeit our communal exploration into the corpse as (a) practical theological matter. We give up the theological significance of our bodies in death if our questions about the corpse can be contained on a simple checklist on a funeral director's planning form.

Our Death Dealing and Our Dealings with Death

There is a popular myth that Americans are beholden to a "death taboo" that keeps us from talking about death, dying, or the dead body at all costs. And *that's* why we can't have substantive conversations about death or the dead body in our communities of faith or with our families.

If you think about it carefully, you can see that this is clearly not the case. Death is everywhere in American society. We watch deaths portrayed constantly on television and in film and video games. We've seen numerous popular television shows that are *about* death like *Six Feet Under* or *Dead like Me* or any number of crime dramas in which each episode is premised on the discovery of a corpse. There have been documentaries about funeral homes like A&E's *Family Plots* or Netflix's *The Casketeers* that treat the funerary work with seriousness while playfully revealing the humorous drama of the owners and employees of the funeral home. Death permeates our culture and consciousness.

We are not held back by a death taboo. What we *do* have is an unhealthy—or at the very least, *unhelpful*—relationship with death. We hold death at a distance by keeping it out of our everyday conversations with friends and family and faith community. We look *at* death rather than talk *about* death. We sensationalize death by portraying it in the media through violence and gore, visualizing types of deaths that most of us will never experience. Rarely do our media portray death in the ways that death normally occurs for most of us—cancer, heart attack, old age, stroke, or mundane accident. And we add to the human experience of death all of the maladies of our culture's rampant consumerism and individualism, using money and consumption to further distance ourselves from death's proximity through capitalistic intervention.[26]

Our relationship to the dead body and the myriad pastoral and practical theological questions that this relationship presents also exposes our relationship with death itself. Nothing quite signifies death like the presence of a dead body. And our dealings with the corpse illuminate our dealings with death. Particularly illuminating are situations in which our conventional practices of disposition of the corpse are disrupted.

How we relate to the bodies of our dead when death has occurred beyond the limits of what we would consider a *good* death is an important concern. A practical theology of corpse care explores the materiality and meaning of the dead body and our relationship to it.[27] There is something telling about our visceral reaction to the desecration of a corpse, or even to situations in which the dead body remains uncared for because of situational factors that stretch our funerary practices and professionals to their limits. Our responses to these situations suggest something about our collective sense of significance bound up with the *bodies* of the dead.

Death and the treatment of the dead body are both concerns that loom large in our collective consciousness. Whatever our attitudes toward the corpse, our glib statements do not capture the materiality and meaning of the corpse within the collective consciousness. These popular sentiments, though frequently spoken, are not true to our sense of what a corpse means to us and how we desire to relate to it.

All the biggest questions we are grappling with as a planetary human community are questions that relate in one way or another to the corpse and our relationship to it: environmental ethics in the Anthropocene, lethal police violence against Black bodies, living and dying amid a worldwide pandemic, the commodification of everything within the neoliberal economic order of global capitalism, practical theological questions about the materiality and meaning of the dead body.[28] It becomes clear that a checklist on a funeral home's disposition form falls short of helping us get at these vital questions.

The questions posed by the corpse—and questions about death writ large—are experiencing a time of great ferment. Examples of this changing relationship to death and to the corpse are visible in the popularity of death cafés throughout North America, the rise of the green burial movement from the Deep South to the West Coast, and the increasing interest in DIY home funerals and in burgeoning alternative methods of body "disposition" beyond burial or cremation.

Yet Christian communities are largely missing from this movement. We have abdicated our historic role in care for the dead to a funeral profession-*cum*-industry. We have stopped reflecting on the revelation of a body once that body no longer bears life. We have submitted our care for the dead to the simplicity of a checklist of disposition options, and we haven't adequately queried these options' histories, their attachments to power, and their implications in the larger web of life. We have not equipped our communities of faith to be truly faithful to one another all the way to the end of this embodied life.

One day we will all become dead bodies.

With this book, we stake our claim that this fact of our embodiment, this incarnational truth, this process of our bodily becoming, is a practical theological question par excellence.

1

The Corpse

From Antiquity to Antebellum Garden Cemeteries

The Corpse in Antiquity

To UNDERSTAND THE attitude(s) toward the deceased among the first Jesus followers in particular, one must understand the issue within its larger Greco-Roman context. At one end of the spectrum is the well-known and generally accepted view that the proper disposal of a corpse was an essential (filial) obligation in antiquity among Jews.[1] The larger plot of Sophocles's *Antigone* also turns on filial responsibility to bury the dead. The proper treatment of corpses has been explored in the extant written record at least since Sophocles's tragedy, in which the protagonist, Antigone, defies royal decree in order to bury her brother, Polynices, by sprinkling dust over his corpse. Corpses deserved proper disposal. But the manner of disposal could vary. Lucian observed, "The Greek burns, the Persian buries, the Indian encases in glass, the Scythian eats, the Egyptian salts."[2]

Despite this widespread commitment to proper burial in the ancient world, the concern for corpse care was not universal. Diogenes, a fourth-century BCE Cynic philosopher who questioned cultural conventions and norms, famously informed his friends "that they should throw him out unburied, that every wild beast might feed on him, or thrust him into a ditch and sprinkle a little dust over him. But according to others, his instructions were that they should throw him into the Ilissus, in order that he might be useful to his brethren."[3]

This attitude was not limited to pagan traditions. Jesus himself, when confronted by a would-be follower with the excuse, "Lord, let me first go and bury my father," responded, "Let the dead bury their own dead."[4] To be sure, while both Diogenes and Jesus call for a certain neglect of corpse care, their motives are drastically different. Apparently, Diogenes desired to be reunited with the natural world as part of the cycle of life, while Jesus's call to "leave the dead to bury their own dead" turns on the fact that the filial duty to bury a parent, while sacred and significant, must submit to a higher and more urgent call to follow Jesus. In that sense, the good must yield to the best.

If disregard for the corpse lies at one end of the spectrum in antiquity, preoccupation with the deceased lies at the other.[5] None were more notorious for their attention to the corpse in their practice of embalming than the Egyptians.[6] The Egyptian practice of embalming led in some quarters to accusations of necrophilia or purported sexual encounters between the living and the dead.[7] Herodotus, in the midst of his detailed account of the practice of embalming, comments on measures taken to discourage such acts: "Wives of notable men, and women of great beauty and reputation, are not at once given to the embalmers, but only after they have been dead for three or four days; this is done to deter the embalmers from having intercourse with the women. For it is said that one was caught having intercourse with the fresh corpse of a woman, and was denounced by his fellow-workman."[8]

Also on this end of the spectrum are reports about, and accusations of, necromancy, which abounded in antiquity. Strictly speaking, necromancy referred to interrogating the dead concerning information about the future.[9] The most famous account in the biblical tradition describes Saul's attempt to call up the spirit of Samuel through the medium of the witch of Endor, but such stories were common in the ancient world.[10]

Despite the variation in views of the corpse and its requisite care, there was, at least among the elite in imperial Rome, a fairly consistent and widespread notion of what a "good death" comprised:

> When death was imminent relations and close friends gathered round the dying person's bed, to comfort and support him or

> her and to give vent to their own grief. The nearest relative present gave the last kiss, to catch the soul, which, so it was believed, left the body with the final breath. The same relative then closed the departed's eyes . . . , after which all the near relatives called upon the dead by name . . . and lamented him or her, a process that continued at intervals until the body was disposed by cremation or inhumation. The next act was to take the body from the bed, to set it on the ground . . . , and to wash it and anoint it. Then followed the dressing of the corpse—in a toga, in the case of a male Roman citizen, the laying of a wreath on its head, . . . and the placing of a coin in the mouth to pay for the deceased's fare in Charon's barque. All was ready now for the body's exposition.[11]

The surviving written records of Roman funerals typically describe those of Roman elites, while all of the characters with mentions of burial rites in the New Testament would be classified as nonelites.[12] Nonetheless, the idealized Roman "good death" provides a more ready and accurate benchmark than would the default cultural knowledge of, or experience with, notions of the "good death" among modern readers.

Corpse Care among Jesus Followers

No New Testament writer devotes more attention, however inadvertently, to details of death rites than does the author of Luke/Acts. For this reason, the Lukan corpus provides a convenient, if fragmentary, glimpse into funeral rituals among the early Jesus followers.

In order to have a corpse, one must have a death, and there is no dearth of deaths in Luke/Acts. It is, however, surprisingly difficult to assess an accurate "body count" in the Lukan corpus. There are at least four recorded deaths in the Third Gospel: the son of the widow of Nain,[13] John the Baptist,[14] the unnamed father of Jesus's would-be follower,[15] and Jesus.[16] If one counts Jairus's daughter (who Jesus says is only "sleeping"[17]), the eighteen upon whom the tower in Siloam fell, and the unspecified number of Galileans slaughtered by Pilate,[18] then the number goes up significantly. In Acts, there are nine reported deaths: Jesus;[19] Judas;[20] Ananias and Sapphira;[21] Stephen;[22] Tabitha;[23] James, brother of John;[24] Herod;[25] and Eutychus.[26] In addition, there is in Acts an unspecified number of followers of the Way who died during Saul/Paul's persecution of the Way.[27] It is from this "death database" that we will construct a taxonomy of corpse care rituals.[28]

Washing the body. In Acts 9, the narrator recounts the story of the death and resuscitation of Tabitha/Dorcas, a disciple in Joppa.[29] At the beginning of the story, the narrator records that Tabitha "fell sick and died; and when they had washed her, they laid her in an upper room."[30] Luke does not recount at first who performed the act of washing the corpse, but one might surmise from details given later in the story that the corpse care team consisted of some of the widows, who were grieving Tabitha's death (and who had been the recipients of garments made by Dorcas when she had been among them).[31] Later Jewish texts attest to the ritual of washing the body: "They may make ready [on the Sabbath] all that is needful for the dead, and anoint it and wash it, provided that they do not move any member of it."[32] This story in Acts may be the earliest reference to this Jewish practice,[33] but the practice in antiquity was not limited to Jews, at least according to literary references. Homer reports that Achilles ordered the washing of Patroclus's corpse before burial.[34]

Anointing the body. While there are no instances of actually anointing a corpse in Luke/Acts, it was the intention of the women to anoint Jesus's body when they approached his tomb on the first Easter morning.[35] Anointing was also apparently a practice among Jews in the Second Temple period. The *Testament of Abraham* reports that a multitude of angels "tended the body of the just Abraham with divine ointments and perfumes until the third day after his death."[36] Anointing the corpse often accompanied its washing in both Jewish and Greco-Roman sources.[37]

Swaddling the body. Joseph of Arimathea took charge of Jesus's body and, after its deposition, "wrapped it in a linen cloth."[38] In Acts 5, Luke reports that "the young men came and wrapped up his [Ananias's] body, then carried him out and buried him."[39] The wrapping mentioned here, hastily done, may not have the same ritualistic connotation as the "enshrouding" imagined in later Jewish texts, but it shares the same purpose of bestowing dignity upon the corpse.[40] Once again, the treatment of Patroclus's corpse included covering or wrapping it in soft linen.[41]

Processional with the body. Luke 7 describes a funeral procession in Nain for the only son of a widow.[42] Jesus encounters the procession at the gate of the city.[43] Presumably, the son's body was being transported outside the city for burial. Jesus stops the procession and touches the "bier," which is being carried by an unspecified number of pallbearers.[44] Luke does not specify the number or identity of the bearers, but based on ancient literary evidence, the authorial audience might have imagined them to be male relatives or friends or (perhaps less likely, given the presumed social status of the widow, who had lost her only son) newly liberated slaves.[45] Generally, the number of bier bearers was four, though among some elite families, there may have been as many as eight.[46]

Burying the body. Responsibility for burying the corpse was generally understood to be a filial duty.[47] That view is presumed in the request of Jesus's would-be follower to be given permission to bury his father, even though Jesus rejects the request.[48] In the absence of family members or financial resources, friends of the deceased might assume this responsibility.[49] Thus, a wealthy acquaintance, Joseph of Arimathea, requests and receives Jesus's corpse and has it inhumed in a "rock-hewn tomb."[50] Luke's authorial audience in the larger Greco-Roman world might have viewed the Jesus followers through the lens of a Greco-Roman voluntary association and thus understood Joseph's gesture as an obligatory action on behalf of the emerging "Christ-group."[51] Likewise, the church takes responsibility for the burial of its members Ananias and Sapphira even when its members have betrayed the community.[52] Luke remarks, in passing, that the couple are buried beside each other, presumably in a freshly dug trench pit, familiar to "lower-class" Jews and gentiles alike.[53] The audience may have filled the gaps in the Stephen scene in the same way: both for those "devout persons" who buried Stephen (e.g., read through the lens of voluntary associational obligations) and for the (unnamed) locale of his burial (a trench grave).

Mourning the body. Mourning was a central feature of deathcare in antiquity. Lucian's description of burial practices is skeptical but instructive nonetheless: "Then they wash them, as if the lake in Hades wasn't big enough for people there to wash in! Then having anointed the body, which is already speeding to decay, with fine perfumes, and crowning it with beautiful flowers, they lay the dead in state, dressed in splendid clothes, which are probably thought to stop them getting cold on the journey, and from being seen naked by Cerberus. Next come cries of distress, wailing women, weeping everywhere, the beating of breasts, tearing of hair and blood marked cheeks."[54]

Nevertheless, "mourning customs differed from one place to another no less than burial customs themselves, though some elements were widespread among Mediterranean cultures."[55] The ideal among Roman elites was for women to serve a leading role in mourning the dead, though there is evidence that Roman elite males were criticized for a lack of expressed grief in certain contexts, especially during the imperial period.[56] Luke records mourning at the deaths of Jesus ("all the crowds . . . returned home, beating their breasts"[57]), Stephen (over whose death "loud lamentation" was made[58]), and Tabitha (the "widows stood beside him [Peter] weeping").[59] Excessive mourning might be discouraged, as it was in some philosophic texts and in later rabbinic tradition.[60]

Cremation in imperial Roman corpse care was a variation on inhumation. Ashes were often buried in sarcophagi. Eventually, the dominant Roman practice returned to inhumation as a gentler and more humane way of disposing of the dead. Roman dead were viewed organically as eating and being eaten (hence, the term *sarcophagus*: "flesh-eater"). Libations were poured, and food was left at graves. Christians at first opposed the Roman funerary meal. But by the fourth century, they celebrated the Eucharist in graveyards, a practice that continued until at least the fifth century.[61] Despite the assured results of older scholarship, however, there is no indication before the medieval period that the church provided official burial sites—cemeteries—for the communal burial of Christians.[62]

Corpse Care in the Middle Ages

In the context of third-century persecutions, the Christian body was in danger of mutilation and dishonor. Resurrection was viewed as "victory over putrefaction as well as justice for the deceased in burial and reassemblage of the mutilated body."[63] Christians were not the only ones concerned with the practice of dividing and moving the corpse; Roman culture had strong taboos against such cadaver violations. By the twelfth century, however, the partition and distribution of Christian bodies was widespread.[64] The corpses of Christian saints were regularly eviscerated, deboned, or boiled to provide relics for veneration. Such practices were not the result of denigration of the body but rather the outcome of the recognition of the importance of the body to the self. At the same time, the import assigned to the corpse was at the price of denying its decay as a natural and organic process. Thirteenth-century orthodox writers accused "heretics" of viewing the body as rot and decay. Technical and arcane debates over the nature of the resurrected body raged during the thirteenth and fourteenth centuries and had a profound impact on Christian views of the corpse and its care.

Later reflections on this period led to the conclusion that by the fourteenth century, "a modified version of Greek dualism triumphed in Western Christian theology. . . . The immortal soul became the container and guarantee of what we mean by self."[65] Recent reassessments, however, suggest that these discussions of the resurrection body seem "to have been about the body—about the horror and the glory of the physical stuff in which humans feel, suffer, experience the world, grow and give birth, decay and die."[66] The actual practice of corpse care in the medieval period narrates a different account than that of the dualistic victory of soul over body. The intimate connection between the material and resurrected body underpinned the "incorruptible" bodies of saints, a view that reached back into the second century, when the body of Saint Cecilia (d. 177) was venerated as incorruptible, and included a number of medieval saints, including, inter alia, Saint Etheldreda (d. 679), Saint Cuthbert (d. 687), and Saint Catherine of Siena (d. 1380).

Furthermore, the integrity of the material body to the resurrected body gave moral warrant to divide and distribute the dead bodies of saints as part of the dissemination of the self. Some bodies were embalmed to preserve the shape of the self; others were partitioned for burial in various sites; still other "holy bodies" were opened for interior secret signs of sanctity analogous to the external sign of stigmata. Parallel to these activities among the religious were the introduction of dissection into the medical school anatomy curriculum and the rise of postmortem autopsies (to determine the cause of death in legal cases), both in Bologna in the late thirteenth and early fourteenth centuries. No one during this period "suggested that the corpse was merely a husk left behind."[67]

The Colonizing Corpse and the Corpses of the Colonized

When European deathways[68] arrived on the North American continent, there already existed pluriform ways of imagining and ritualizing death and tending to the dead among Native Americans. While these deathways are a potent source of wisdom in and of themselves, this section looks at the contact between Native American and European deathways in the earliest days of colonization and the ways that the corpses of the colonizers and the colonized became active participants in relationships of both cooperation and violence between Europeans and Native Americans. The deathcare practices of the Indigenous people of this land became a point of deep interest for the colonizers and an important point of contact between Europeans and Native Americans.

This exploration raises important questions about *what the corpse can do* in its relationship with the living and with the larger ecological web of life and in what ways the corpse can become a mediator of *harm* and *healing* among living communities. The picture that develops here from the earliest contact among Native American, African, and European deathways contributes to the critical assessment of the notion that the contemporary conventional story of our relationship with the bodies of the dead can, or should, be encapsulated within a broadly predictable chain of events.

Native American Deathcare

Prior to European colonization of North America, the burial practices of Native Americans in what became known as New England largely involved burying bodies directly in the ground, about three feet deep, without adornment of the body and absent the presence of grave goods (personal possessions or items of significance buried with the body for the deceased to carry into the afterlife).[69] Knees of the deceased were drawn upward toward the chest, and the body was placed on its side. Archaeological evidence suggests that most burials of this pre-sixteenth-century era were single burials rather than burials in a designated burial ground.

After European contact with fishermen and traders began, however, Native burial practices began to show evidence of increasing change. Native Americans began burying the dead in burial grounds containing several hundred interments. Grave goods from both Native and European sources were buried with the bodies of the dead, which were now adorned with bracelets and armbands with more frequency.[70]

Roger Williams, colonist and progenitor of Baptists in America, held a deep interest in Native American languages and culture and noted many practices. He observed in his book *A Key to the Languages of America* that the Narragansett people had multiple words to describe the dying process: "He is not yet departed," "He is drawing on," "He cannot live long," "He is near dead," "He is dead," "He is gone." Williams also observed that the deathbed scene was important for Native Americans—as it was for Europeans—and that women played a central role at the bedside of the dying.[71]

One of the most important aspects to note in the developing story of relationships with the bodies of the dead is those points at which the predictable narrative is disrupted. While some very small changes in Native American burial practices may be attributed to contact with colonizing Europeans (e.g., European-made grave goods buried with the deceased), European diseases brought about the most palpably significant rupture in Native American deathcare.

In 1618, a series of epidemics ravaged the Native American people of New England, potentially reducing the population by up to 90 percent, setting off a "mortality-induced chaos" and leaving survivors unable to tend their dead.[72] As will be clear throughout this developing narrative of our relationship with the corpse, nothing bespeaks absolute chaos in the lives of a people like unburied corpses, the dead left untended by the living.

Missionizing with the Corpse

One reason that we know far less about early deathways of enslaved people is the lack of missionary interest in Christianizing Africans and African Americans in the earliest days of slavery, in stark contrast to the missionary efforts among Native Americans. The relations between slaveholders and enslaved people were more exploitative than the relationships between Europeans and Native Americans. Slaveholders did not need to understand enslaved people in order to extract their labor. Settlers did, however, need to understand Native Americans in hopes of forging alliances and gaining land in the colonies.[73]

The French Jesuits in New France developed a strategy for converting Indigenous people to Christianity that focused on the centrality of the deathbed scene. Sharing similar ideas with the Native peoples about the importance of the sacredness of human remains made the connection over deathways a central point of interest between the Catholic missionaries and the Indigenous people of Canada. Responses to the missionary efforts were mixed, some adopting Christianity and Christian deathways, others refusing, and others drawing on the knowledge of Catholic deathways to further resist colonization through corpse desecration.[74] Nevertheless, the centrality of the deathbed scene and the trial of death was of vital importance to the missionary efforts: "A glorious death . . . was the best proof of missionary success. Dying speeches also had the advantage, from the missionaries' standpoint, of being irrefutable."[75]

Weaponizing the Corpse

In a context of violence—through both invasive colonization and extractive enslavement—the corpses of the colonizers and the colonized were regularly weaponized. Christina Sharpe says, "We must think through containment, regulation, punishment, capture, and captivity and the ways the manifold representations of blackness become the symbol, par excellence, for the less-than-human being condemned to death," not only in the historical record, but also in the ongoing reappearances of these realities in contemporary prisons and schools.[76] Bodies regularly become sites of violence, and the fact of a body's death does not remove that flesh from the prospect of being enlisted in waging war.

Native Americans used knowledge of European deathways as a weapon against the colonizers, just as colonizers used their knowledge of Native deathways as a bludgeon against Native Americans. Corpse mutilation was a horrifying prospect for Europeans—a theme that will arise again in the ongoing narrative of relationships with the corpse into the nineteenth century. Native Americans learned this through extensive contact with the deathways of Europeans in the early colonies of North America and employed methods of "postmortem humiliations" in conflict with colonists. Similarly, enslaved Africans drew upon this knowledge in rebellions against their enslavers.[77]

The bodies of Native American dead were important mediating figures between the ecological landscape and the human community. This is one thing that the English and Native Americans held in common. Many of the English, too, saw a sanctifying function of the dead placed in the landscape, though for the English, this belief was held more particularly for those killed in an important cause like war rather than for the bodies of the dead more broadly.[78]

Understanding this connection, the English used the destruction of Native burial grounds and temples as a tactic of colonial violence in an attempt to rupture the relationship of the Native communities with the land in which the bones of their ancestors were interred, thereby severing the connection between people and land.[79]

English accounts of battles with Native Americans focused heavily on the corpse: violations of the sanctity of corpses through mutilation and the denial of burial for the English dead. These images of rotting and mutilated corpses became synonymous with the perceived "savagery" of Native peoples and fueled the rage of the English against Native Americans.[80]

European colonizers were not unaccustomed to corpse mutilation of their own enemies, however. For the English in particular, the mutilation of corpses had a long association with state-sanctioned violence that included heads placed upon poles, genitals cut off and thrown to pigs, limbs severed from bodies, and disinterment of corpses for those who could not be adequately punished for their supposed crimes in life and were therefore subject to desecration in death. Politicized corpse desecration occurred among both Catholics and Protestants in England.[81]

In another sense, however, Native Americans drew upon the power of their own dead in their ability to fight colonization. Algonquians in both the Carolinas and Virginia found death rituals an important means of cover for the gatherings of warriors as well as inspiration for the mission of the men who were going to war.[82] Their death rituals contributed to the preservation of their lives against colonial violence.

Far from inert and anything but meaningless materiality, the corpse played an active role in the earliest contact among Native Americans, Africans, and Europeans. Intentional and violent interference with the relationship between the living and the bodies of their dead has a long imbrication with narratives of colonization and the control of living populations, as "the political order has depended on trampling over the bones of indigenous peoples and glorifying the remains of figures whose significance reflects the principles and mission of the nation."[83]

Sharpe poses a further question in this context of violence: "What does it look like, entail, and mean to attend to, care for, comfort, and defend, those already dead, those dying, and those living lives consigned to the possibility of always-imminent death, life lived in the presence of death; to live this imminence and immanence as and in the 'wake'?"[84]

This narrative strand connecting the corpse with control will continue to weave its way through the story of our relationship with the bodies of our dead in both overtly violent and seemingly innocuous ways.

The Puritan Corpse

Death was ubiquitous from the outset of the colonization of New England by the British. In 1620, after their landing at Patuxet (Plymouth), nearly half of the Separatist colonists died over the course of the first winter. An "evangelism of fear positioned the realities of death at the center of communal life" in New England.[85] The Separatists and Puritans brought with them the death rituals of their communities in England, though very quickly their practices surrounding death began to take a different shape.

In England, Puritans held an admixture of fear of death and reserved hope (*not assurance*) of the soul's fate in heaven. The body, on the other hand, was theologically of little importance to the Puritans—a husk that the soul leaves behind. Puritans wrote of the corpse as a horror to behold and an abhorrent spectacle. Certainly, no attempts were made to preserve the corpse as had been the practice of others in the past and would be for later generations in the New World. For the Puritans of England, the funeral was of little religious value, and when in control of the government, they made regular attempts to remove the handling of the dead from the purview of churches and place it into the charge of civic government.[86]

Funerals for the English Puritans were austere occasions with very little ceremony. A funeral sermon was more a sermon that happened to be preached at a funeral rather than having anything to do with the deceased person's life or the meaning of death. And the extreme anti-Catholic views of the Puritans meant no Christian iconography adorned the tombstones of English Puritan burying grounds.[87] Such iconography smacked of Catholicism.

For those early Puritans who made their way to the New World, these austere practices of deathcare endured for a time. But very quickly, this ascetic scene of deathcare changed dramatically. By the mid- to late seventeenth century, there was a boom in expensive deathcare trappings and elaborate funerary ceremonies among the Puritans of Boston.[88] Many social, cultural, and psychological theories exist to explain this change.

Stannard suggests that a prime cause of this shift in deathways is attributable to the Puritans of New England taking on a cultural and psychological identity of their own that was increasingly distinct from their former feeling of unity with the Puritans of England. Now feeling on their own, new deathways emerged for the Puritans of New England.[89]

As customs of funerary ritual developed, the relationship between the bodies of the living and their dead was characterized by intimacy, close proximity, caring activity, and physicality. Those closest to the deceased prepared the body for burial. Caring for the corpse in the home was the primary purview of women in the family.[90] After the body was washed and prepared, the corpse would often be laid out at the home of the deceased or at the church in which the deceased was a member while funeral preparations were made. Notably, church business would continue undisturbed by the presence of the corpse lying in the midst of the congregation.[91]

This picture of early American deathcare evinces "a valuable, and vital, social relation" between the living and the dead.[92] The diary of Samuel Sewall (1652–1730), for example, details his experience of nearly two thousand deaths and hundreds of burials in the span of fifty-five years. Sewall made periodic visits to his own family's tomb in Boston's Granary Burying Ground to check on the condition of the tomb and its occupants. He described at various points needing to bury the scattered bones and pieces of coffins from long-decomposed family members entombed there and even moving bodies from place to place when newly deceased family were to be entombed within.[93]

The accouterments of death became elaborate and expensive as the seventeenth century progressed. Gloves were sent to friends and others in the community as an invitation to the funeral—sometimes with glove quality indicating the status of the invitee. The community would be summoned to the funerary proceedings by the ringing of the church bell (verboten by the Puritans of England). Gloves, scarves, mourning ribbons, and cloaks were worn by those in the procession, with members of the deceased's community taking turns carrying the coffin to the grave.[94] The coffin—a staple technology of deathcare—had advanced by this point in Puritan history too: made of quality wood (which was difficult to come by in England but plentiful in the colonies), lined with cloth, and covered in a heavy mort-cloth, often with pinned-on funeral verses written by those close to the deceased.[95]

After the funeral, the community returned to the church or home of the deceased for a feast and were often gifted gold funeral rings inlaid with the typical Puritan death iconography in black enamel—death's-heads, skeletons, and coffins.[96] In engraved form, the corpse remained present in the death rituals of Puritans of New England. These reminders of the fleeting nature of life would similarly adorn the grave markers in Puritan burial grounds when stone markers became more common in the mid-1650s, with further reminders of one's impending death through messages like *memento mori* (remember that you must die) and *tempus fugit* (time flies).[97]

While we often imagine that the elaborate and expensive funeral is a modern American creation, Puritan funerals—even for the wealthiest of the dead—could cost up to 20 percent of the deceased person's estate. Even in the early 1700s, this fact disturbed some clergy and politicians alike. Cotton Mather expressed his growing hesitations about the ostentation and expense of funerals in 1713, and in 1724, the Massachusetts legislature passed an act restricting the extraordinary expense of funerals.[98]

In stark contrast to this growing reality in New England, it took much longer for funerals to take on this type of cultural importance in places like Virginia and New York, where the New York legislature had to pass an act *requiring* that some attention be given to the burial of the dead due to the neglected nature of deathcare there. The law required that a delegation of neighbors view the deceased and proceed with the corpse to a gravesite to ensure it was properly buried.[99]

Already in this era, we see class becoming a central issue in who gets what treatment in death. But even more so, the interjection of funerary accouterments and public display begins a long process of decentering the corpse from its role in the process of deathcare. Elaborate processions through the city streets drew in numerous citizens with no connection to the deceased, and the spectacle of mourning itself—with all its ornate trimming indicative of one's socioeconomic status in life—became central.[100] Mourners began displacing the dead at the center of urban deathcare.

The influence of Puritanism decreased over time but maintained a degree of cultural and intellectual influence well into the eighteenth century.[101] In the 1720s, however, a more optimistic sentimentality surrounding death began to displace the Puritan drama over death's inevitability and the uncertain prospect of where one would spend eternity. Stannard describes it this way: "The shift here from fearful anticipation to eager longing of death, though not always so dramatic, runs through virtually all the available materials on death and dying during this period, from poetry to sermons, from journals to sepulchral art."[102] Death's-heads gradually morphed into softer, more cherubic winged heads.

Changes in funerary customs and deathcare rituals are not easy for any society to make. They emerge in response to the questions that communities of the living are asking about their collective life together and reflect the changing values and meanings of the larger society. As a cultural separation from their English counterparts emerged and the cities within the colonies grew, funerary practices emerged in response to questions of family, religion, urbanization, class, and collective identity that would develop across the centuries into an identifiable "Americanization" of the corpse.

The Urban Corpse in Nature

The family was the clear locus of authority over care for the corpse in the centuries leading up to the early 1800s. Though, as we've seen, both church and government intervened in various ways to shape care for the dead.[103] As of yet, there was very little involvement of deathcare "professionals" in the practices of tending to the dead. But a period of intense ferment in deathcare practice took shape in the early to mid-nineteenth century, setting trajectories of deathcare that are followed to the present day. Over time, "the corpse was transformed from a sacred object exclusively within the interpretive jurisdiction of religion into a symbolic commodity on the marketplace of ideas."[104]

More and more, deathcare became a concern for public health officials, legislative bodies, an emerging class of professionals in the undertaking business, and an industrious class of deathcare technology inventors.[105] The hearse and the coffin both became business ventures, helping families get their dead where they needed to go with a new sense of funerary style developing in the early nineteenth century. Coffins emerged as *caskets* with a far more elaborate design and a new name to denote the "preciousness of the remains."[106]

The most significant change in our relationship to the dead during this era, however, was the movement of urban dead out of the cities and into surrounding rural landscapes. The first of the rural cemeteries, or garden cemeteries, in the United States is Mount Auburn Cemetery in Cambridge, Massachusetts, founded in 1831, with other cemeteries patterned after it arising in cities across the United States. For example, these include Philadelphia's Laurel Hill Cemetery (1835), Brooklyn's Green-Wood Cemetery (1838), Louisville's Cave Hill Cemetery (1846), Atlanta's Oakland Cemetery (1850), and many more. Mount Auburn Cemetery was the first American burial ground given a proper name.[107]

In an era before urban public parks, which began in the ensuing decades, or the national parks (beginning in 1872), the rural cemetery was a landscape of relationship among the living, the dead, and the web of life that invited visitation, immersion, and meaningful connection. Outside of the city, yes. But not so far outside of the city that working people couldn't visit with regularity—in addition to being buried there.[108]

Mount Auburn's predecessors in the minds of its founders were English gardens and Père-Lachaise Cemetery in Paris. But while the English gardens were for the elite, Mount Auburn was intended for all. And while Père-Lachaise smacked of vanity in its memorialization of men and the celebration of progress, Mount Auburn foregrounded horticulture and celebration of the landscape.[109]

But the rural cemetery was not an innovation in deathcare that came from nowhere, and it is connected in many ways to shifts in our relationship with the dead more broadly rather than simply related to their new places of interment. One must ask *why* these changes took place. After all, among cultural practices of any given community, practices and rituals surrounding death are typically the slowest to change and the most recalcitrant in the face of new possibilities.[110]

Population booms were one impetus for changes in American deathways in the century leading to the turn of the nineteenth century. Throughout the 1700s, the population of New England doubled nearly every twenty to thirty years and was concentrated in cities and towns along the Atlantic. Wealth, too, began to become concentrated as land grew scarce and the commercialization of the economy intensified. Likewise, populations of the poor were growing in these burgeoning US cities.[111]

In the decades following the War of 1812, Boston doubled its population, growing from 33,250 in 1810 to 70,000 in 1830.[112] City center burying grounds, like Boston's King's Chapel (started in 1630), Copp's Hill (1660), and Old Granary (1660) were cramped in the midst of burgeoning American cities, full of the urban dead and unable to expand due to the surrounding city infrastructure. By the early 1730s, burials in these grounds were often taking place four bodies deep as well as in common trenches, and family tombs were often sold to another family after the original family died out.[113] Two of these burying grounds, along with the Central, or Common, burying ground on the edge of the Boston Common, were closed to new burials by ordinance in 1826.[114] New places for the dead were desperately needed.

Physician John Gorham Coffin (1769–1829) issued *Remarks on the Dangers and Duties of Sepulture* to colleagues in Boston arguing for the removal of current urban burials into a suburban locale. In Coffin's vision, the grounds would be extensive and would allow for single burials that permitted a natural process of decay, using only shrouds for the dead that decomposed easily, and the disinterment of bones after a sufficient period of time so that the grave could be used again. "The physician advocated naturalism and simplicity as essentially American, democratic, and anti-aristocratic" and suggested that choosing this new site of burial for the city's dead was a choice for democracy, natural law, and the will of God over against aristocracy, superstition, and human pretensions.[115]

Another impetus for the rupturing of eighteenth-century deathcare narratives was the growing hygienic movement that associated noxious smells with the spread of disease prior to the development of germ theory. The rise of scientific approaches to the corpse and public interest in the science of disease created a sense of danger in relation to the dead body. However misguided that perspective may have been, the corpse was imagined as a source of harm to the living community.[116] The most appealing space for the dead became a "natural" setting outside of daily city life with plentiful room for burial of the dead rather than the burgeoning city centers that had long situated repositories of the dead alongside the dwelling places of the living.

Technologies of deathcare like the hearse for carrying the dead and the carriage for transporting mourners allowed for a lengthier transport than had been possible when walking on foot and carrying the dead upon the shoulders. Hearses were introduced in Boston in 1796.[117] So the possibilities for burial places proliferated as means were created to transport bodies with greater ease, no longer by foot on the shoulders of community members.

The young history of the nation had much to do with the impetus toward memorialization as well. Erecting sites of memory to recall "great men" invoked the practice of memory in order to construct a history for a relatively new nation. The rise in individualism also brought with it a desire to be *remembered* in death, not buried anonymously or in burying grounds that no one would visit, places now seen as repulsive. This was in sharp contrast to the Puritan ideal expressed just a century earlier by Increase Mather (1639–1723), who said, "To praise the dead is to praise corruptible flesh. . . . To praise memory is to worship the dead."[118]

Along with memory, a central impetus of the new monument-laden rural cemetery was patriotism. In the same era when monuments were erected to remember significant figures, battles, and wars, the graves of historic figures became sites of memory for a nation in the process of constructing its history.[119] Additionally, the monuments of the new cemetery were believed to hold the potential to instill ambition in those who visited the graves of heroes among the dead. And beyond patriotic heroes, those like minister William Ellery Channing were also committed to celebrating those of personal virtue and those who lived lives in service to the community.[120]

It was in this period of ferment, too, that the corpse became medicalized. Dissection of the cadaver became a staple in anatomical training for medical doctors. The medical gaze increased understandings of disease and addressed anew the many mysteries related to death. However, most Protestants looked upon the prospect of dissection of the corpse with disgust and revulsion as an act of destruction of both the corpse itself and the memories of those still living.[121] "Resurrectionists," men who would steal corpses from the grave for medical doctors to use in training, became a problem in the nineteenth century when the corpse took on a particular value for the growing medical field.[122] While this violated a sense of sacredness of the body at rest in death, at the same time—perhaps with a little imaginative distance from the realities of corpses considered to be "our own"—there was an increasing interest in literature featuring the "opening, destroying, and peering inside" of corpses.[123]

The Industrial Revolution provided yet another force in the changing deathcare landscape in the nineteenth century. Industry began to exert a forceful grip on our relationship to time. The compartmentalization of work, a longer workday in an industrial context, and a new relationship to time (and productivity) measured by the factory clock meant that caring for the bodies of their own dead—as had been the unquestioned norm in previous eras—was no longer possible for many urban workers.[124] This precipitated a gradual removal of death from the everyday lives of the living and an absconding of the corpse from the care of family. Care for the bodies of the dead was being given over to a nascent class of undertakers, not yet a full-fledged profession but on its way to becoming so by century's end.

But in some ways, the developing rural cemetery—in its movement from the industrializing cities to rural pastoral landscapes—subverted this grip on our relationship both with time and with the dead by connecting people in new ways to the past as well as to the future. The rural cemetery's joining of kin across time—both biological and chosen kinship associations with revered community figures—connected people with a larger communal network that spanned temporal distance. And on a human timescale, the seeming timelessness of the "natural world" fostered a complex relationship with deep time that expanded imagination beyond the one-dimensional relationship with now dominant machines.

Joseph Story, Supreme Court justice and ardent supporter of Mount Auburn Cemetery, makes this connection among the dimensions of the ecological, the anthropological, relations with and across time, and health/healing clear in his dedicatory speech at the cemetery. He notes the scenery of this new place of repose of the dead—"the hill and the valley, the still, silent dell, and the deep forest"—urging listeners to climb to the highest point in the cemetery from which they could view the Charles River, "with its rippling current, like the stream of time hastening to the ocean of eternity." He continues,

> If there are any feelings of our nature, not bounded by earth, and yet stopping short of the skies, which are more strong and more universal than all others, they will be found in our solicitude as to the time and place and manner of our death; in the desire to die in the arms of our friends; to have the last sad offices to our remains performed by their affection; to repose in the land of our nativity; to be gathered to the sepulchres of our

> fathers. . . . Dust as we are, the frail tenements, which enclose our spirits but for a season, are dear, are inexpressibly dear to us. We derive solace, nay, pleasure from the reflection, that when the hour of separation comes, these earthly remains will still retain the tender regard of those whom we leave behind;—that the spot, where they shall lie, will be remembered with a fond and soothing reverence . . . and our kindred in remote generations feel that a local inspiration hovers round it.[125]

Story then reaches deeper into human history, appealing to the history of humanity and the commonality shared in these sentiments among the "aboriginal Germans," the Egyptians, the Hebrews, the "ancient Asiatics," the Greeks, and the Romans.

The old, austere burying grounds constructed a particular relationship with death and the dead. Not visited as sites of memory, they were replete with symbols of death's inevitability, and with no attempt at beautification, the confrontation with death in these burying grounds was stark and frightful. The new rural cemeteries constructed a different relationship with death and the dead. The relationship of the living with the bodies of the dead was now being connected with a relational kinship with the dead through the evocation of memory, and a new type of relationship between the landscape, with its healing and revelatory potential, and the bodies of the dead interred within arose.

Also around the mid-1800s, postmortem photography became popular, with the dead photographed and sometimes posed with the living members of the family. These were often the only photographs a family had of a deceased loved one given the rarity and expense of the new photographic technology. Some estimate that in the 1840s, photography of the dead outpaced wedding photography at a ratio of three to one.[126] Even as the corpse began to depart the home and even the city, images of the dead graced mantelpieces and adorned walls. In the rural cemetery, in literature, and in photographic depictions, there was beauty in death and even in the corpse itself.

Iconography on the grave markers of rural cemeteries evinced the new emotional relationships being cultivated with the dead: from death's-heads and skeletons and hourglasses running out of sand to melancholic images of lanterns and obelisks, urns and willows. The gray slate of the Puritan burying grounds was replaced by the white marble of Mount Auburn, symbolizing these emerging new attitudes toward death. Though the cemetery itself was committed to a nondenominational identity, these grave markers, once stark reminders of one's own death, transformed into hopeful signs of the heavenly salvation being preached by more liberal expressions of religion like Unitarianism and Universalism.[127]

Even when religion is not in the foreground, it is always in the background of our relationships with the bodies of our dead. Within transcendentalist thought, "death was understood as an opportunity to move beyond the confines of the material world and into a more liberated and holistic form of existence."[128] The body in death could be embraced by nature, and the body as a material container for the soul could maintain a connection to the spiritual significance now located in "nature" in the growing religious sentiment of the day.

The corpse itself, once a site of religious instruction and missionary efforts among early Puritans in the colonies, was now losing its significance in the religious imagination of the nineteenth century. The spirit and the afterlife rose to prominence in religious teaching and preaching on death.[129] Thus, changing emotional responses to the dead influenced how communities tended to the corpse. As the Puritan emotion of fear in the face of death waned, ministers of growing liberal traditions helped reshape an emotional response to the death of loved ones. A reserved hope of the soul's salvation in Puritanism was replaced in liberal traditions by a greater assurance in the prospect of eternal salvation.[130]

Even with an increasing focus on the life of the soul in death, the death of the body was still very much on the minds of Mount Auburn's founders.[131] There was no attempt to cover over the fact of death and attending decay with new, more sentimental, more hopeful funerary iconography. Take, for example, the consecration hymn sung by the two thousand attendees at Mount Auburn Cemetery's opening, written by Universalist minister and Hollis Professor of Divinity at Harvard John Pierpont (sung to the tune of "Old Hundred," to which many Protestants sing the doxology):

To thee, O God, in humble trust,
Our hearts their cheerful incense burn,
For this thy word, "Thou art of dust,
And unto dust shalt thou return,"

For what were life, life's work all done,
The hopes, joys, loves, that cling to clay,
All, all, departed, one by one,
And yet life's load borne on for aye!

Decay! Decay! 'tis stamped on all!
All bloom, in flower and flesh, shall fade;
Ye whispering trees, when we shall fall,
Be our long sleep beneath your shade!

Here to thy bosom, mother Earth,
Take back, in peace, what thou hast given;
And all that is of heavenly birth,
O God in peace, recall to heaven![132]

Cemetery founder and physician Jacob Bigelow also added his perspective on the matter, stating that "the progress of all organized beings is toward decay."[133] There was no attempt to hide death behind the beauty of nature. Rather, the earth itself became the restful home of the corpse in the imaginations of those who cultivated this space of interment for the bodies of their city's dead.

Bigelow, the one to propose a rural cemetery to his influential friends in 1825, gave a lecture on Mount Auburn Cemetery before its opening, in which he said, "The elements which have once moved and circulated in living frames, do not become extinct nor useless after death: they offer materials from which other living frames are to be constructed."[134] Thus, Bigelow considered preservation of the corpse unnatural, though he was keen to preserve memories of the dead. He thought that the brick vaults in graveyards of his era were attempts to divide the bodies of the dead from the rest of creation.[135] This is a notable sentiment from a leader in the rural cemetery movement of the 1830s that would soon be severely challenged in the coming decades.

In an ironic way, removing the dead from the center of everyday life in the city brought people *closer* to the bodies of their dead in repose (though not necessarily in the provision of direct *care* for the bodies of the dead). Whereas the city-center burying grounds were not places frequently visited and were seen by most in the nineteenth century as putrescent eyesores, people *did* visit Mount Auburn in droves—from Cambridge and Boston, from all over the United States, and in the thousands from Europe. Most people were simply not accustomed to visiting the graves of loved ones when Mount Auburn was founded, an infrequency that has returned today in most cemeteries across the United States. But the founders of the cemetery were convinced of the power held by the natural landscape to provide salve for the grief of mourners and those needing an escape from the urban setting[136]—a belief far removed from that of John Wesley (1703–91), the founding figure of Methodism, who feared that landscapes like the English gardens upon which Mount Auburn was styled would seduce people into pantheistic idolatry of nature.[137]

As the rural or garden cemetery emerged as a popular and lucrative alternative to the crowded city burying grounds, the private corporations that started, owned, and ran the new cemeteries all over the East Coast also gained power over the dead in the forms of standardizations of practice and regulations concerning disposition.[138]

While the urban circumstances are important in narrating this relationship with the bodies of our dead over time, this is not a single story. Not everyone lived in a city in proximity to a new rural cemetery. The developing religious perspectives and sentiments about the relationship among the living, the dead, and nature were not monolithic. Outside of the burgeoning cityscape and its new rural resting places, the ground into which frontier communities placed their dead took on special significance for the identity of the nation as well. The frontier dead marked conquered space that helped tell the story of American expansionism. Harkening back to earlier contact between European colonizers and Native peoples, it was only the white corpse that was afforded the respect of bodies marking space as sacred—even if in a secularized, nationalistic sense. The Native corpse was something less than human remains in the eyes of frontier settlers and was thus susceptible to disturbance and desecration.[139]

The orderly placement of the corpse into a location within the frontier landscape is related not just to the expansion of European-descended settlers farther into the American West. This placement of bodies also relates to a developing white American relationship to "nature." The wilderness had to be vanquished and nature tamed, and the living—as well as their dead—cultivated conditions amenable to settlement and expansion. So too in northern Protestant communities, the placement of the dead into an ordered site with appropriate ceremony became a way of negotiating the "boundary between nature and culture."[140] But as we will see, that was not the only boundary that loomed large in the minds of early nineteenth-century Americans.

2

The Corpse

From the Civil War to the Industrialization of Deathcare

The Racialization of Corpse Care

When the slave trade started bringing Africans to the shores of North America, enslaved peoples brought with them their deathways and relationships with the bodies of their dead. The earliest practices of deathways among enslaved Africans are an important part of understanding the relationship with the corpse in twenty-first-century America. While Europeans were largely disinterested in the deathways of Africans, the knowledge that they did gain over time made way for the enslaved corpse to become a means of intimidation. African deathways—like European deathways—held a sense of sacredness for the corpse itself and expressed a deep respect for the bodies of the dead. Violating this sense of sacredness and respect through deprivation of funeral rites and burial, burning or decapitating the bodies of dead enslaved people, and forcing the enslaved community to witness the desecrated corpse all became means of control. These methods were perhaps most notable as a means of preventing the "escape" of enslaved persons through suicide, as it was known among slaveholders that many Africans believed they would return to their homes in Africa after death. These were not just practices of corpse violence implemented by independent slaveholders but also practices of corpse desecration that were sanctioned by the state in a number of cases.[1]

The forced movement of enslaved people from the African continent to North America brought with it a rich practice of deathcare. While slaveholders were far less interested in documenting the practices of Africans brought to North America than early settlers were in studying the deathways of Native Americans, what is clear is that care for the dead was of central importance to Africans brought to the colonies.

The people of the Gold Coast in West Africa washed the bodies of their dead prior to wrapping the bodies in cloth, with assembled family and friends sprinkling ashes on the shrouded bodies of their dead. A funeral procession to the grave included singing, weeping, and beating on metal basins while the body, bound to a board, was carried to the grave. Some were buried in burial grounds and others beneath the floors of their own homes. Grave goods were left on top of the grave rather than inside it. And families celebrated the departure of their beloved into the afterlife with funeral festivities after the burial and memorialization practices to remember their dead in the extended period that followed.[2] In the case of burials of family members beneath the floors of the home, "the presence of the dead was quite literally unavoidable, as the very earth beneath one's home became a sacred space of remembrance."[3]

Slave ships became the first site of ruptured deathways for the enslaved people of West Africa. Mortality rates on the arduous trip across the Atlantic in packed ship holds were enormous, and many Africans were separated from the comfort of historic deathcare rituals through burial at sea, as ships were followed across the ocean by schools of sharks.[4]

Slaveholders on plantations were largely disinterested in the spiritual lives of enslaved people, which allowed for a degree of autonomy for the enslaved when it came to burying their own dead. Yet from accounts from plantations in the Caribbean and some Moravian missionaries—some of the few early missionaries interested in evangelizing enslaved people—the picture of deathcare among enslaved people on plantations demonstrates necessary augmentations of that of their homeland. Cloth for shrouds was rarely available, coffins were uncommon, and evening burials were typical, possibly so as not to interfere with their enforced labor. But many aspects of West African funerary rituals continued: singing, dancing, and loud noises accompanied the body to interment. And while most plantations had ground set aside for burial of enslaved people, some continued to bury their dead nearer to their living quarters.[5]

In some contexts, slaveholders were responsible for the provision of a coffin and, in some cases, even purchased gravestones for enslaved people, either as a gesture of reward or as a sign of the slaveholder's own wealth.[6] In some of the graveyards of enslaved people, placing grave goods like rocks, shells, and broken plates and pottery belonging to the deceased became a practice in continuity with burial traditions in Africa.

Notably, while white burial customs seem to have very little influence on the early years of slavery burial traditions in North America, some white southerners *did* seem to find inspiration in African and African American burial practices in the nineteenth and twentieth centuries, leaving seashells, jars, and wine bottles on the graves of their own kin, reminiscent of the African tradition.[7] And we know of at least one account of an enslaved person's burial that stoked admiration and inspiration in the heart of a British naval physician named George Pinkard, who recorded that rather than shoveling the dirt roughly onto the body, the community he observed burying their dead in Barbados placed the dirt into a basket and gently emptied it into the grave—a practice he commended to his British countrymen.[8]

Two prominent themes arise in the relationship with the corpse among the colonizers and the colonized. First, the deathways of Native Americans and enslaved Africans became an important point of *missionary* interest—though not to the same degree—among Christian colonizers. Second, the corpse served as a *weapon* of violence for Europeans violently taking land from Native Americans and forcibly removing bodies from Africa to the colonies of North America. All the while, Native Americans and Africans / African Americans developed practices of corpse care that were congruent with their historic deathways, could incorporate new practices when desired, and were capable of accommodating adverse circumstances when imposed.

Just as in an earlier era, the care of the dead was a vital act of autonomy for enslaved people undergoing the violence of the plantation, and burial of the dead in the nineteenth century provided a degree of autonomy, freedom, and status to African Americans in a segregated society of racialized violence. Funerary and mourning traditions have been, from the start, a vital component of Black life in the United States.

Poet Claudia Rankine once asked a friend what it was like being the mother of a Black son. Rankine's friend replied, "The condition of black life is one of mourning." Liberal white people, Rankine says, can feel temporarily bad about Black suffering, but "no mode of empathy . . . can replicate the daily strain of knowing that as a black person you can be killed for simply being black."[9] This sentiment was true in the seventeenth century and continues to be true of the Black experience in the twenty-first. And the violence of racism that denies the autonomy of so many Black bodies, even in death, was paramount in the care for the African American corpse in the nineteenth century.

While Mount Auburn Cemetery in Cambridge was open to all races for burial from its consecration in 1831—and many of Boston's African American lawyers, musicians, authors, and businesspeople are buried there—racial segregation was the more common practice in America's cemeteries.[10] It is important in narrating a relationship between communities of the living and the bodies of our dead that we attend to the ways the problems of the living, like racialized violence and segregation, impinge upon our care for the dead. Equally important is how caring for the dead can become an expression of *resistance* to death-dealing social injustices.

For one look into these practices of resistance in African American deathcare, *another* Mount Auburn Cemetery becomes significant—this one in Baltimore, Maryland. Baltimore's African Burying Ground, founded in 1807 by Sharp Street Memorial United Methodist Church, was a place for both church members and the larger African American population of Baltimore, both free and enslaved. Prior to this, African Americans were buried in two of the city's potter's fields, in cemeteries for enslaved people, or in church graveyards—none of which were places *chosen* by African Americans of the city for their burial.[11] According to Kami Fletcher's historical work on this site of Black funerary significance, Baltimore's African Burying Ground "actualized black autonomy in death."[12]

In 1839, the African Burying Ground became Belair Burial Ground, Sharp Street Cemetery in 1871, and finally Mount Auburn Cemetery in 1903. There is much of significance in the history of Baltimore's Mount Auburn. With a long history of enslaved people in rural Maryland being buried in slave cemeteries, separated from the graves of white slaveholders on land owned by white families and in graves rarely marked with anything but wooden markers, the founding of an autonomous African burying ground by an African American church for use by Baltimore's Black population was monumental. Its founding ran against a long history of colonial racialization of deathcare and denial of legal rights to burial plots and freedom to operate burying grounds. Fletcher further suggests, "The burial ground's development maps against an effort for autonomy in death that ultimately fueled cultural and financial autonomy for the collective black community."[13]

Additionally, the burying ground preserved a history of Black life in Baltimore in an era when unmarked burying grounds often succumbed to the erasure of white supremacist history, and it signaled a history in death for those buried there that was separate from imposed inclusion on the margins of the burying grounds of white people. In urban settings in which enslaved people were buried with their white slaveholding family, the enslaved people's graves were often at the opposite end of the lot and were sometimes facing away from the white family.[14] At what became Mount Auburn Baltimore, white bodies were conspicuously absent altogether.

Ownership of the land for one's burial plot became an expression of some degree of freedom in a Jim Crow era when land ownership was often denied to many African Americans. Fletcher notes, "This burial plot of land was their legacy. It allowed these black women, men, and children to be remembered the way they wanted to be remembered. . . . Sharp Street Cemetery memorialized black people's kinship bonds and not their relationships to whites."[15]

It was in this same era of increasing African American autonomy in the care of their dead that President Andrew Jackson signed the Indian Removal Act into law in 1830, the year before the Mount Auburn Cemetery in Cambridge was founded. As some African Americans were gradually gaining markers of citizenship and freedom through the ownership of grave plots and the operation of autonomous cemeteries, Native Americans were being driven from the land that held the bones of their ancestors. The act allowed for the forced expulsion of Native tribes to land west of the Mississippi so that white settlers could claim Native ancestral lands, initiating a march to the west that we know as the Trail of Tears. As geographer Laura Harjo notes, "Mvskoke people were not afforded the time or permission to bury their dead; the most they could do was take their relative to the side of the trail and cover the corpse with rocks and a blanket. But by taking care of their kin who died along the trail in this way, Mvskokvlke created sacred places along the route to present-day Oklahoma, and along the way produced ephemeral spaces."[16]

Thus, the founders of Mount Auburn in Cambridge were celebrating the sacred merger of the dead and the picturesque landscape, and the African Burying Ground (soon to be known as Mount Auburn in Baltimore) provided important portents of autonomy and freedom to African Americans interred in land that was finally *theirs*. Meanwhile, Native Americans in the United States were sacralizing land on routes carved by white settler colonialism, oppression, and violence by interring the bodies of their dead in unmarked graves in uncelebrated landscapes made no less sacred by the bones of ancestors who died along the way.

Our interactions with the bodies of our dead are shot through with connections to time (both past and future) and relationships to space (that of the burial place as well as other sites of memory). It is also evident in the narrative thus far how intimately connected our corpse care practices and the body's final disposition are to relationships to kin, both human and within the larger web of life. In a long and complex history, whites, African Americans, and Native Americans held the place of burial of the dead as a location of both sacred importance and secular meaning.

Significant shifts in our relationships with the bodies of the dead occur when taken-for-granted associations between the living and the dead are ruptured: through colonial violence, changing religious landscapes, shifts in literal landscapes of interment, and reclamation of autonomy over the care of our dead. One rupture in the nation's historic narrative of relationship to the bodies of the dead precipitated a rift between the living and the dead in such a significant way that it would change our relationship with the corpse for the next century and a half: the Civil War.

The Traumatized Corpse

Leaving the place of one's birth and never returning is a common experience for many contemporary Americans. Before the 1800s, however, it was a rarity. The living stayed close to their family graves and would know that one day, they would be buried alongside them. Burial in the rural setting occurred on family farms or in county graveyards or local churchyards. Burial grounds in early American cities were either at the center or just on the periphery of the living community. For most of human history, death was a near and familial phenomenon, and corpses never resided too far from the locale of the living.

Americans' current high rate of contemporary preference for dying at home has a long history. Until the nineteenth century, the dead largely resided near the living in both urban and rural landscapes. Our not-too-distant relatives cared for the dying in their family homes, corpses were washed by the loving hands of relatives, members of the community carried the deceased on their shoulders to their place of interment, and everyone walked by the graves of their community's dead on the way to nearly every place they went. Up to this point, "burial was an intimate affair in which the living were familiar, both physically and imaginatively, with the dead" in rural American life.[17] Even up to the first decade of the twentieth century, fewer than 15 percent of Americans died away from home.[18]

The ideal death—the "good death"—suggested a person should die at home, surrounded by loved ones at the deathbed. Family members witnessing the death held the responsibility of assessing the state of the dying loved one's soul. Last words were heard with anticipation and held with a sense of reverence and truthfulness:[19] "The teachings that last words imparted served as a lingering exhortation and a persisting tie between the living and the dead."[20]

During the first half of the nineteenth century, however, this began to change, even in more rural locales. People became more mobile and less likely to be present to attend their family graves. Thus, the country graveyard began its process of becoming a socially secured space tended less and less by families of the dead. The ideal was dramatically and traumatically ruptured beginning in 1861 with the onset of the Civil War.

The trauma of the Civil War and its effect on the relationship of the living to the bodies of the dead cannot be understood without a clear sense of the preceding antebellum relationship to the corpse. In the period prior to the war, a person was intimately tethered to their own body after death, remaining as a presence in close association with the body-now-dead until after the funerary rituals ushered the dead out of the presence of the living. The corpse was a liminal being, "unstable, indeterminate, and ambiguous," that needed an intimate relationship with the living in order to get where it needed to go, from preparation of the body to burial in its grave.[21]

During the war, people died away from home, outside of the care of family and community, in the hundreds of thousands: "The integral relationship between the body and the human self it housed was as shattered as the wounded men."[22] A belief in the physical resurrection of the body called for sacred care for the corpse.[23] Yet eyewitnesses to the field hospitals' piles of amputated limbs and photographs documenting the dead strewn across battlefield after battlefield called into question the corporeal resurrection of the dead in the theological imaginations of Americans living far from sites of war. In many cases, care for the bodies of the dead was an impossibility: "There were simply too many of them to accommodate time-consuming reflection and proper, respectful treatment."[24]

At times, bodies were left on the battlefield unburied by the victorious army, which was soon on the move to a different site of conflict. When graves were dug, the bodies of one's comrades received a simple yet individual burial, whereas enemies were often buried in large pits, though at times mass burials were all that could be managed for the dead on both sides. More than 40 percent of the Union dead and many more Confederate dead—hundreds of thousands of men—were interred on the battlefield without names.[25]

Chaplains in the Union and the Confederacy replaced families as holders of the sacred duty of helping soldiers die well, or as well as possible under the circumstances of war.[26] Nurses, too, assisted in the good death by notating the last words of soldiers dying in field hospitals and sending them home to families awaiting word. Personal possessions became representations of lost loved ones when bodies were not recoverable.[27] The religious faith of the dying that could be observed by family at the bedside was replaced by patriotism, and courage evidenced by soldiers dying in battle replaced the observation of the death scene.[28]

Though race holds an obvious place in considerations of the Civil War, it played another role in the care of the dead. During the war, the Union assigned African Americans to burial detail for the Union dead prior to their later admittance into the fighting regiments.[29] This was gruesome and grueling work on battlefields strewn with the dead. On the Confederate side, enslaved people who had accompanied

Confederate officers into war were often the ones who retrieved their bodies and brought them home to mourning white families.[30]

In modern times, the United States spends more than $100 million each year trying to find and identify the nearly eighty-eight thousand military members still missing from World War II, the Korean War, and the Vietnam War.[31] But this desire for the recovery of the dead from battlefields is not new. One testament to the importance of recovering a body and maintaining proximity to the physical remains of the dead during the Civil War is the fact that many families who could afford to do so flocked to battlefields where a loved one had died in an attempt to recover the body *themselves* and bring the loved one's corpse home.[32] Another is the effort to rebury the Civil War dead who did not receive proper burials during the war. In the North, this was the work of the army and the federal government. In the South, this was the work of the people, "a grassroots undertaking that mobilized the white South in ways that extended well beyond the immediate purposes of bereavement and commemoration."[33]

As is often the case, when desires are left unmet, there are industrious and inventive people who step forward with marketable practices for answering these unmet desires. In the case of the thousands of men dying away from home for the first time in American history, embalmers answered the most pressing question on the minds of many devastated families: How can we gain proximity to the bodies of our dead?

The grief-desire for a body to handle and mourn superseded the disgust most northerners held for manipulation of and invasive interference with the body, and embalming was accommodated as an acceptable practice for the preservation and transport of the body back home for those who could afford the new technology.[34] Until the Civil War, embalming was a practice relegated to the cadaver labs of medical schools to preserve corpses for dissection.[35]

The lack of a body to mourn through the typical "manipulation" of deathcare at home added to the trauma of the Civil War more broadly for families who lost loved ones on the battlefield. This pervasive lack of a dead body led to practices of ultramanipulation through embalming. The modern practice of embalming described later in this chapter has not changed in its very basic features since the Civil War: it was a process of using arteries and veins to replace the body's natural fluids with preservative fluids in order to slow the process of decomposition.

What became a *choice* for many white Protestants of some means during and after the war was often *forced* upon those who ended up embalmed on a medical school cadaver dissection table. These were, namely, the working poor, immigrants, and African Americans. Among those outside of the wealthier classes, embalming and dissection remained an undesirable fate for the bodies of the dead even after the war.[36] Race and class have long influenced what is done with/to the bodies of the dead and who gets to make such decisions.

What had taken place largely in secret in the laboratories of schools of medical training was now brought into public consciousness during the war as a technology that promised the return of loved ones from the field of battle for those who could afford it. With the advent of embalming as an increasingly common practice during the war, it was a *technology of deathcare for the wealthy.* The poor of the Union simply could not afford it and were left with a physical absence in their mourning where a body should be.

Field embalmers often followed troops from battle to battle, offering their services to those not fortunate enough to make it out alive. After a soldier left the embalming table, he could be placed into a coffin and put onto a train headed north, back to the care of families awaiting his return. The most famous Civil War embalmer, Thomas Holmes, embalmed more than four thousand soldiers at a price of one hundred dollars each, becoming a wealthy man in the aftermath of the war.[37]

Before the war's end, there were many advertisements for the miracles of embalming, some of which very clearly played on racial prejudice, linking decay and race. An 1863 advertisement in a Virginia newspaper taken out by Dr. F. A. Hutton, for example, read, "Bodies Embalmed by us NEVER TURN BLACK!"[38] The physiological process of decomposition, changing the color of the skin to darker and darker hues, reminded some of the very markers that differentiated race.[39]

It is nearly impossible to imagine the enormity of the trauma created by death in the Civil War. It is not difficult to empathically imagine the particular trauma of death without a body. We might think of the bodies painstakingly recovered from the attack on the World Trade Center in 2001, or the many missing in action from America's numerous wars, or Indigenous people who go "missing" and are never recovered, or those who died in the Covid-19 pandemic away from families who could not attend the bedside of the dying or attend funerals for their dead. But it is hard to imagine 620,000 people dying of disease and on battlefields away from home in a country in which dying *at home* was the taken-for-granted norm.

Embalming in the context of the Civil War was a trauma practice—meeting the relational needs of families whose loved ones were dying away from home in vast numbers for the first time in American history. But it is a lingering question why Americans of this era didn't see embalming and transportation of the body back home from the battlefield as an extreme stopgap measure designed for a specific purpose and period. A number of factors perpetuated this practice far beyond its *extreme necessary usage*, carrying it all the way into our current *conventional* deathcare practices in the twenty-first-century United States.

During the timespan of the Civil War, embalming the bodies of our dead went from an anathematized practice of gross interference with the corpse to an accepted practice of preservation that was no longer resisted but *desired*. Thus, a new class of professionals was charged with care for the dead, administering a new technology in relation to the corpse. Embalmers became "people who could, in effect, domesticate the corpse for the public imagination and assume managerial responsibilities for its disposal."[40] This shift toward a public embrace of the technology of embalming and the professionalization of deathcare would have been impossible to imagine without the trauma of Civil War death and the ways it worked on the imaginations of Americans—particularly northerners—in relation to death and the bodies of their dead.

The chance to view their dead—to have close proximity to the bodies of their loved ones once again—eased the distaste for embalming and created an opening in the psyche traumatized by war. Embalming became acceptable as a wartime necessity for those who could afford it. Why it then became *preferable* in the period after the war is another question. Important to note in this developing narrative of our relationship with the bodies of our dead is that the practice of embalming quite suddenly shifted responsibility for care of the corpse from familial and community care to the care of professional strangers, and it instituted a shift from a history of deathcare leadership exercised by women of the household to the charge of professional men with specialized technology and marketable deathcare skills.[41]

The Civil War indelibly changed Americans' relationship with the corpse. Practical considerations of caring for the dead on battlefields far from home, the sheer number of dead often requiring anonymous mass graves, and death at a distance from family and friends to attend the bedside of the dying all contributed to a divestment of relational attachment to the bodies of dead loved ones.[42]

The decreasing importance of the corpse also held practical effects for those charged with fighting the war, too, as "severing the body from any spiritual and symbolic associations allowed the machine of war to operate more smoothly and efficiently."[43] The United States Sanitary Commission was charged with this psychic severing of the living from their dead in order to bolster the efficiency of the Union in winning the war. The very meaning of death and Americans' relationship to the bodies of the dead became a tool for fighting the Confederacy. The commission worked toward a "disciplined disinterest in dead bodies" and a "regimented pragmatism in their disposal" in order that sentiment, piety, and religious reverence for the bodies of the dead would not get in the way of Union soldiers' ability to fight the war.[44]

By the end of the Civil War, the government's keen interest in the pragmatic treatment of the war dead and the psycho-spiritual trauma of mass battlefield death depicted in photographs and felt in the homes of myriad Americans solidified a shift toward state and professional usurpation of care for the corpse, which once rested in the hands of familial relations and religious authorities.

Adding to this relegation of the corpse to the margins of funerary praxis, the spirit usurped the body in Protestant theological approaches to the dead, beginning before the war and cemented in the theological imagination in the decades after. The dead person's spirit and its place in the afterlife became of central concern, and the corpse retained little value in the Protestant mind.[45] Thus, religious instruction no longer centered on the corpse, and families abdicated the care of the bodies of their dead. The corpse lost much of its imaginative potential; what it gained were economic value and professional oversight.

Professionalized Deathcare and the Commodification of the Corpse

Prior to the Civil War, deathcare practices were already shifting to adapt to the aesthetic tastes of the upper and middle classes. Liverymen were employed for transportation of the corpse. Simple coffins were replaced by ornate caskets of stone, marble, glass, bronze, and other metals. But the "business" of deathcare, as it was clearly becoming, was not yet standardized. It was a "fragmented, disorganized, and irregular" practice of service persons who were not yet a deathcare "industry."[46] But the industry was well on its way.

The first national meeting of funeral directors occurred in 1882, and it was clear from the outset how the emerging profession saw its work: the preservation of the body was at the center of the work and would become the priority of corpse care in America.[47] Embalmers, cabinetmakers fashioning coffins, and carriage drivers helping with the transport of the dead had been at work since the Civil War. But only in the 1880s did this loose confederation of *men* begin to see themselves as part of a profession that would grow into a massive industry within the century.

The final gaze at the body of a dead loved one is a consistent desire of Americans and a feature of our attitudes toward death that has had staying power throughout shifting relationships with the corpse.[48] During the centuries when people nearly always died at home, families provided care for their own dead, the community got the corpse to its place of burial, and seeing the corpse of a loved one was an unquestioned reality. As medical care became more sophisticated, hospitals increasingly became the place of death for many into the early twentieth century. As the deathbed was exiting the home, so too the corpse was moving out. When death and the dead exited the family home and professionals took charge of the corpse, provision for the final gaze at the dead loved one became the centerpiece of the new profession of undertaking.

Embalming was presented to a public only beginning to overcome an aversion to invasive manipulation of dead bodies. Into the 1930s and through the 1950s, funeral directors appealed to psychology to justify the need for a viewable body, potent in its healing potential for mourners.[49] Both psychologically and spiritually, the family's ability to view the embalmed corpse in the death space of a funeral parlor became "the active agent in the eventual triumph over the pain of losing a loved one."[50]

It is important to note, though unsurprising, that funeral homes throughout the early and mid-nineteenth century were sites of racism and segregation. Black clients at white-owned funeral homes were treated as second class, having to use back doors and basement entries, and Black corpses were regularly disrespected by white funeral professionals. When Black men entered the funeral industry, they were often subject to violence for diverting income from white funeral directors.[51] As in an earlier era, when funeral rituals were autonomous activities for enslaved people on the plantation and Black-owned cemeteries became portents of freedom for African American communities, "the black undertaker emerged as a businessman in a community of few independent black-owned businesses."[52] It was both a business opportunity and an occasion to provide care for a community subjected to racialized violence and discriminatory practices even in death.

Embalming, too, became a regular practice in African American funerals. Not only the visible presence of the corpse at the funeral but a tactile engagement with the body through laying on of hands and kissing and expressing one's grief over the body of a loved one were important in Black funerary traditions. The presence of the body of the dead held emotional power, harkening back to West African traditions noted earlier.[53]

The funeral itself was a means of expressing the worth of a life not often accorded value in a white supremacist culture. Karla Holloway says, "For many it was important to note the procession of cars and prominent numbers of mourners. Their visual excess expressed a story that African America otherwise had difficulty illustrating—that these were lives of importance and substance, or that these were individuals, no matter their failings or the degree to which their lives were quietly lived, who were loved."[54] For both community members of prominence and those less celebrated, the funeral was a sacred undertaking, and Black undertakers were now caring for their own community's dead in greater numbers.

This shift to professionalized deathcare for a dead body that held marketable value marked the modern era of corpse care: "No longer an emotional time to wallow in suffering and sorrow, the moment of death, according to modernists, should be a time of certitude, self-control, and objective rationality."[55] What was, just decades earlier, an anathematized process of invasive manipulation of the bodies of the dead was now a lucrative practice increasingly desired among Americans.

The new profession also made an appeal about the dangers of the corpse to the public that took eventual shape in state laws and legal cases giving more and more control of the dead over to the funeral profession.[56]

Much like in the early nineteenth century's crowded urban burying grounds, when the dead were moved to the outskirts of the city, the dead body at the turn of the twentieth century became, in the minds of many, an object of danger and harm that required professional and technological intervention to render it safe, approachable, and viewable. It is remarkable to note how relatively quickly this sanitary sentiment came about when just a generation or two earlier, families regularly cared for their dead in the home, from the time of death through to interment. But the corpse was no longer a domestic concern.

The typical American funeral home in the late nineteenth and early twentieth centuries resembled a private home. It provided a space of intimacy with the dead removed from the *actual* home but retained many of its homey qualities. But as Gary Laderman notes, "Imagery associated with funeral homes also called upon another sacred American institution to evoke feelings of trust, respect, and honor: the church,"[57] and "funeral directors became the new priests who presided over the corpse—that object abandoned by traditional religious authorities and community networks."[58]

When caring for the corpse became a business opportunity, the centrality of women in the domestic order of deathcare shifted to a gendered division of labor with men in charge of the now lucrative preparation of the dead.[59] But a new division of labor in caring for the dead took shape in the early 1900s between ministers and the newly emerging funeral profession. Some ministers were disturbed by the new emphasis placed upon the treatment of the corpse, the centrality of the embalmed body, and its expense and cautioned against purchasing expensive caskets, flowers, and grave markers. Many pastors resented the now secondary role they played in the funeral, with the entire affair often planned with funeral directors before involving the minister. Yet others welcomed this new role, encouraging trust in funeral directors and supporting their charge over the bodies of the dead. Particularly among Black funeral directors and ministers, the relationship between the pastor and mortician, the church and the funeral home, became one of close association, as each institution was thoroughly segregated, and each professional provided critical services to members of their community from birth to death.[60]

In the ensuing decades, however, funeral directors began to push beyond the charge of the corporal components of deathcare to advocate for their role as grief specialists.[61] Today, many funeral directors undertake the National Funeral Directors Association (NFDA) "Certified Celebrant Training" to become skilled in "ceremonial writing" and performance as a "master of ceremonies." The NFDA describes its perceived need for this emerging role in this way: "As families' wishes continue to evolve, it is more important than ever to offer a variety of services that meet their needs and exceed their expectations. Fewer families are incorporating religious rites into memorial services—how do you fill that gap? Many funeral homes look to Celebrants and find it most economical to train their staff to accommodate this growing demand for customized services. A Certified Celebrant works with the funeral director to provide a funeral service, memorial service or tribute that is personalized and individualized to reflect the personality and life-style of the deceased."[62]

The ongoing decrease in Americans' involvement with religious institutions and contact with local clergy who can be called upon to officiate at funerals of loved ones is giving rise to the fulfillment of ritual and ceremonial roles by the funeral director, who is now becoming a one-stop shop for every aspect of deathcare, from the corporeal to the spiritual.

The Corpse in Flame

What the late eighteenth century was to embalming and the shift of the dead into the hands of professionals, the early twentieth century was to shifting the dead from the dirt to the flame. Prothero makes the helpful connection between contemporary conventional burial (i.e., an embalmed body within a casket and a vault) and cremation by saying, "Both burial and cremation as practiced in the contemporary United States respond to decay by forbidding it, via either embalming or incineration (or both)."[63] Both hide from the eyes of loved ones the changes that occur in the body in the hours and days after death by either preserving the body through the injection of carcinogenic fluids and the application of cosmetics or totally incinerating the flesh.

In addition to burial among many tribes, some Native Americans had also practiced cremation for centuries. The first cremation of a white person in the colonial era was that of a prominent colonel and merchant from South Carolina named Henry Laurens, who, afraid of being buried alive (a common fear when he died in 1792 and into the next century), chose to be cremated in the open air on his Charleston estate.[64]

Open-air cremations, while common in other cultures, were not typically practiced in America. The modern iteration of cremation began in 1876 in a structure specifically built for the purpose in southwestern Pennsylvania. This soon led to the first publicly run crematory in New York City, which opened in 1889. But the way in which cremation came to be practiced by more than half of Americans—likely three quarters within the next decade—is a more complex story. Having a professional place the body of a loved one into flame—a body solicitously cared for in death by family members just a half century before—was not an easy sell in the earliest days of cremation's emergence on the deathcare scene.

There is a disturbing association between the dead body and the immigrant body in the early history of American cremation. Immigrants and the dead were both regular scapegoats in the urban sanitary reform movement. The arguments for the removal of the corpse from the city center often mirrored the arguments made about the dangers of disease brought by immigrants to urban life. In the cremation movement, similar sanitary arguments were made, linking the dangers of the dead with the dangers of immigrant bodies. The notion that infectious diseases were imported rather than homegrown appeared with regularity in early cremation advocacy literature. Even the first public crematory in New York City was designed to cremate the bodies of immigrants who died of infectious diseases. At the same time, *anti*cremationists used race as a foil for the practice of cremation, spreading tales of the ashes of white bodies being mixed with the ashes of Black bodies.[65]

While we cannot overlook the early association between the supposed dirt and dangers of the decomposing dead and the xenophobic imagination, early cremationists also had loftier notions about why cremation was preferable to burial. Many of the earliest proponents advocated for cremation through a narrative that tied its modern iteration to ancient practices in Egypt, Greece, and India, all the while touting the scientific and technological advances of the modern versions of these supposedly timeless practices.

In a starkly dichotomous way, cremation advocates drew upon a sense of disgust for decay by portraying burial as associated with pollution, uncleanliness, and superstition and cremation with purity, cleanliness, and science. The arguments were regularly anticorporeal, urging consumers not to make too much of the body—as was regularly the case in funerary practice of the day. Notably, African Americans and immigrants were regularly associated with burial in these arguments, representing parochialism and the past, whereas cremation represented technology and the future of deathcare.[66]

Ecological arguments were also employed, stating that cremation was "natural" and, of course, took up no large tracts of land for burial. It is easy to see how compelling this ecological argument would have been in the early nineteenth century before we thought too much about carbon emissions. Today, however, it is important to note that cremation is an energy-intensive practice of body disposition in which the body is subjected to temperatures of 1,400–1,800 degrees Fahrenheit for two to three hours, after which the bones that remain are mechanically pulverized into approximately four to six pounds of remains that are made up primarily of sodium with a very high pH harmful to plant growth. This process accounts for the use of ninety-two cubic meters of natural gas per body, equivalent to a five-hundred-mile car trip.[67]

Theologically, cremation posed a challenge to the notion of a bodily resurrection of the dead. But cremationists had at least two responses to this. First, there should be no difference between the ways we imagine God resurrecting the decomposed corpses of those buried through the centuries and the ways God can reconstitute cremated remains. Second, a more successful argument suggested that the resurrection of the dead was a spiritual, not a corporeal, resurrection.[68] Early on, many liberal religious figures and denominations—notably Unitarians and Episcopalians—expressed support for the practice of cremation. Cremationists were not shy about using theological terms and viewed the crematory as "a last baptism by incandescent heat" and the flame as representative of the Holy Spirit.[69]

In the earliest days, the funerary rites of cremation resembled those of burial. Families were present, and peepholes allowed family to witness the flame. But in the early 1900s, peepholes were covered up, and families were removed from the furnace rooms and moved first into adjacent chapels and much later to columbaria, where ashes were placed and funerary rites performed.

The boom in cremation occurred around 1963. Jessica Mitford published her famed book *The American Way of Death*, excoriating the funeral industry. Cremation was an alternative to the expenses and extravagances of embalming and caskets and burial. The funeral industry, however, was not invested in this shift to cremation. In cremation's ascent to its current popularity, the AIDS epidemic sped the funeral industry's acceptance of cremation. Professionals rarely recommended the practice, which almost always came at a financial loss to the funeral director. In many cases involving a body that died of AIDS, however, the funeral director encouraged cremation.[70] The rise of individualism and the deaths of baby boomers also served to solidify cremation's hold on the deathcare imagination of the nation: "simplicity, spontaneity, informality, flexibility, improvisation, participation, and (above all) personalization" shaped the funeral rites of this generation, and cremation was perfect for the occasion.[71]

In the twenty-first century, cremation is firmly established as a staple of the deathcare landscape, now expressed in increasingly industrialized iterations of care.

The Industrialized Corpse

Deathcare in the United States is a multivalent narrative. But there is a clear trajectory of greater and greater human intervention and attempts to control or outright subvert the process of the body's death and decay otherwise guided by ecological processes. What Dr. Jacob Bigelow touted as the body's natural decay and return to the earth at the founding of Mount Auburn Cemetery in 1831 had become anathema within a century. The staple practices of this trajectory toward our dominant practice today exert extreme control over the corpse, separating it as much as possible from the ecological process of decay and return to the earth by extinguishing the corporeal remains through fire or preserving the body with chemicals and sealing it within a casket and a vault where earthy elements cannot touch it.

What is now largely considered a "conventional" funeral in our contemporary context is one in which the family and community of the deceased surrender complete control and responsibility of the dead body to professionals. Families become guests in the funeral home, where their dead loved one is quasi host, quasi guest. Churches become sites of some aspects of funerary rituals for families who so choose, but even these practices can take place elsewhere and are often directed by funeral professionals.

Whereas the corpse once enjoyed an intimate connection with the family in a caring relationship to the remains of a dead loved one, the bodies of the dead were gradually decentered from the funeral drama and often absent altogether in "a disembodied memorial for the body."[72] The family and larger community of the deceased person became the center of the death drama in America—first as guests in funeral homes, then as consumers of a funeral industry. Professionals came to serve the family as consumers of the goods and services of deathcare. The corpse in this industrialized drama retained a certain kind of spotlight, but it became a commodified object, part of the panoply of purchases made in the aftermath of death.

The rural cemeteries of the early nineteenth century, connecting the living, the dead, and the ecological web, gave way to the lawn park cemeteries of the late eighteenth century. The lawn park was organized for human convenience in neat rows of tombstones. In the early twentieth century, the lawn park gave way to the memorial park, in which monuments are no more and flat stone or bronze markers sit atop graves, flush with the ground; plantings are minimal; and roads cater to the driver rather than pathways to the pedestrian.[73] There is an important connection between the modern memorial park and the grid system of urban design that developed beginning in New York in 1811, soon becoming "the defining spatial feature of American life." Sachs argues, "The grid was both the symbol and the instrument of expansion, speculation, efficiency, economy, uniformity, convenience, rationality, progress" and was employed to transform the landscape despite the features of forests, fields, rivers, mountains, or swamps that may get in the way of said progress.[74] Nothing could be more indicative of the industrialization of deathcare.

While most funeral homes today are locally owned, often by families who have operated them for generations, a dominant force in modern funeral practice arose with the advent of multinational funeral conglomerates. The largest of these is Service Corporation International (SCI), founded in 1963, which owns over 1,900 funeral homes and cemeteries in forty-four states, eight Canadian provinces, the District of Columbia, and Puerto Rico.[75] SCI's most current investor fact sheet reports $3.4 billion in revenue with an estimated market share of 15 to 16 percent of the deathcare business in North America. Their report optimistically states that SCI is the predominant player in the stable funeral industry, giving it a size and scale to provide "significant competitive advantages (purchasing power, shared resources, back-office efficiencies)," and that it is also poised to benefit from the aging of America. Additionally, SCI boasts annual preneed sales (people paying for their funerals before the time of death) of nearly $2 billion through a four-thousand-person sales force with a backlog of future revenues from preneed sales exceeding $12 billion.[76]

There are good funeral directors, caring funeral directors, funeral directors who got into the work in order to help people in their grief by caring for the dead and those who love them. This portrait of the industrialization of deathcare is not an argument against the funeral profession wholesale. This review does, however, present pressing questions about the ills of industrializing practices that gradually serve to disintegrate our connection to central aspects of life. As one parallel among many, the industrialization of food production has disintegrated our relationship with the sources of our sustenance and, through practices of greed, has diminished the capacity of nonindustrial farmers and food producers. What was once a fully integrated relationship with the dead in day-to-day life, an inevitable and unavoidable connection between the community of the living and the community of the dead, is now disintegrated by the commodification of the corpse and the industrialization of deathcare.

The Contemporary Conventional American Corpse

Currently, in the United States, there is an overwhelming preference for death to occur at home, a desire expressed by 80 percent of Americans. Despite this preference, deaths at home are far rarer than our preferences suggest. Approximately 60 percent of Americans die in acute care hospitals and another 20 percent in nursing homes. That leaves only about 20 percent of Americans who experience death at home. A minority of these deaths involve the work of hospice care professionals, often only in the last three to four weeks of life.[77]

This statistical picture is gradually changing, however. When external causes of death (e.g., accidents) are excluded and only medical conditions that lead directly to death are assessed (e.g., heart disease, cancer), the number of hospital deaths between 2003 and 2017 decreased from 39.7 percent to 29.8 percent, nursing home deaths decreased from 23.6 percent to

20.8 percent, and deaths at home increased from 23.8 percent in 2003 to 30.7 percent in 2017. Deaths in hospice facilities increased from 0.2 percent to 8.3 percent in that time frame. As we will see throughout the developing story of the dead body's relationship to the living, social location says a great deal about where one is able to die and under what circumstances. In this study, younger patients, women, and racial and ethnic minorities had lower odds of experiencing death at home than did older, male, and white patients.[78]

When death occurs, whether in a hospital, hospice, or nursing facility or at home, our most typical deathcare scene in the United States today involves a funeral director from one of the country's nineteen thousand–plus funeral homes coming in the hours immediately after the death has occurred.[79] It then begins what one mortuary science professor describes as "a broadly predictable chain of events."[80] After the body of the dead is retrieved by a funeral professional, it is taken from the place of death to a funeral home for preparation, which involves washing the body, massaging the extremities to loosen them up to be positioned in the way they will appear in the casket, and embalming the body.

Statistics are not published on how many of our dead are embalmed every year. And while embalming is not required by law, most funeral homes require embalming if a public viewing is to take place. This is often the case even when a brief viewing is going to occur just before the body is cremated. Embalming takes around three hours and involves the injection of embalming fluid into the carotid artery while, at the same time, the body's blood is drained from the jugular vein. For every fifty to seventy-five pounds of body weight, about a gallon of embalming fluid (largely formaldehyde) is injected. A trocar—a long metal instrument with a sharp end attached to a suction device—is inserted into the abdomen to remove fluids and gasses there. Various other devices and solutions are applied to restore color to the face, keep eyelids and mouths closed, and restore any visible wounds on the body. Hair is groomed and cosmetics are applied, and the body is clothed and casketed.[81]

The preparation of the body eventuates in either burial (practiced in 53.3 percent of deaths in 2010 and projected at 37.9 percent in 2020 and 16 percent in 2040) or cremation (practiced in 40.4 percent of deaths in 2010 and projected at 56 percent in 2020 and 78.4 percent in 2040).[82]

The National Funeral Directors Association lists the 2019 median cost of an adult funeral with viewing of the embalmed body in the funeral home followed by burial in a metal casket inside a burial vault at $9,135. This does not include the cost of a cemetery plot, burial, or a headstone.

The median 2019 cost of an adult funeral with embalming and viewing that is followed by cremation comes in at $5,150. This does not include the cost of the cremation itself, as many funeral homes do not own a crematory, nor does it include the cost of a cremation casket ($1,200) or a basic cardboard cremation container ($150) or urn for the cremated remains ($295).[83] For direct cremation—without the services of embalming, viewing in the funeral home, a cremation casket, and so on—the cost of cremation drops to between $500 and $1,500.[84]

When the body is placed in the ground for burial in our conventional contemporary US cemetery, the corpse, already in a wooden or sealed metal casket, is also placed inside a concrete grave liner or metal vault. The primary difference between a vault and a grave liner is succinctly described by the Pine Hill Cemetery Association: "A grave liner is a reinforced concrete box with drainage holes in the bottom and no seals of any kind. Its purpose is to support the earth around the casket. A vault is also a reinforced concrete box, but has additional polystyrene liners or metal liners inside the box and has butyl seals between the lid and box. They are designed to keep the elements away from the casket."[85] Nearly all conventional cemeteries require the use of at least a grave liner in order to keep the ground from sinking around the casket after the earth settles, making it less laborious to maintain the lawn. Vaults and liners are not, however, required by law. As stated by the Federal Trade Commission, "Outer burial containers are not required by state law anywhere in the US, but many cemeteries require them to prevent the grave from caving in."[86]

As described above, when the body is cremated with flame, it is placed in a cardboard cremation container or wooden cremation casket into a crematory retort—a large furnace—and exposed to heat reaching between 1,400 and 1,800 degrees Fahrenheit for two to three hours, which reduces the body to ash and bone, after which any medical implants like pins and artificial joints are removed and the large fragments of bone are ground down by machine to a finer powder (colloquially called "ashes") and then transferred into an urn or other container.[87] The cremated remains are then returned to the family for scattering, burial, or interment in a columbarium or to be kept in the home.

This rendering of the body's journey to the grave or the crematory after death does not account for the many and varied ways that a death is marked ritually, religiously, and virtually and through gatherings of family and friends. Funeral and memorial services and celebrations of life are often held in churches or funeral chapels or rented gathering spaces. More and more, the body or ashes of the deceased do not make an appearance in these services, though viewings and visitations and wakes in funeral homes are still quite common as well. Families and friends gather for meals, remembering their dead in physical gatherings as well as by posting memorial tributes and messages from friends and family from afar and even lighting virtual candles in online spaces.

This rather succinct process coincides with the typical time frame sanctioned for mourning in the United States. On average, those employed in the United States have a maximum of three days off work to make such arrangements and mourn their loved ones after death.[88]

Most of the details of the conventional deathcare practice in the United States are departures from earlier expressions of deathcare praxis, though they bear similarities to many earlier practices too. Muslim and Jewish practices, in particular, deviate from some of the details in this "broadly predictable chain of events" quite significantly (e.g., typically refusing the practice of embalming). And many other religious and cultural traditions add and subtract and augment these practices. But there is also a type of homogenization that takes place through conventional practices becoming more sedimented in cultures and traditions within the United States in which they weren't originally "conventional," and the funeral industry accommodates many cultural variants into an otherwise rather homogenous process. For example, many crematories are built today to allow a family-witnessed cremation, which is an important part of the deathcare ritual of some cultural and religious traditions.

The Multistoried Corpse

There is no single story of the corpse and our relationship to the bodies of the dead. It is a changing relationship over time and from one context to the next. Questions arise in every era that feel new in that particular time and place, even if they are questions of very old provenance.

There is also no singular ideal for how we will relate to and care for our dead today. The paths forward must address the corpse and our relationship to it anew with returns to old practices as well as the invention of new deathcare technologies.

This effort requires questioning the taken for granted and becoming curious about the entangled relationships that come to the foreground as a result. Deathcare practices change for specific reasons in light of particular questions being asked among communities of the living. The following chapter will develop a practical theological perspective on the entanglements of human communities, technologies, the ecological web of life, and the corpse in light of our own contemporary questions. The purpose of the exploration is not to land on one set of practices that are preferable for everyone. Rather, it is to proliferate possibilities for better practices that arise from the entanglement of relationships in our living and our dying at this particular moment in time: the Anthropocene.

3

The Corpse in the Web of Life

A Practical Theology

We are all dying. We know that much. But we are also *all* dying, not just each one of us, but the whole of humanity along with myriad other species in what many now casually call the sixth mass extinction.[1] According to a 2019 report of the 145 scientists writing for the United Nations Intergovernmental Science-Policy Platform on Biodiversity and Ecosystem Services, around one million of the earth's eight million species are threatened with extinction due to climate and ecological destruction caused by humans.[2] This is the context in which we must reconsider our relationship to the corpse: a mélange of human-induced factors of ecological destruction and climate change now being written into the geological record, an era many now term the Anthropocene.[3]

Death may be the last vestige of material evidence to speak against the ideology of human supremacy over the rest of the earth; the corpse itself is a material reminder of our entanglement within the vast web of life on the planet. Unlike many of our ancestors, we have largely stopped thinking about the body when it dies. We have given that aspect of our life and death over to a professionalized chain of events that we think very little about, necessitating scant personal involvement if we so choose. We have certainly not made of the corpse a site of *theological* curiosity or revelatory potential. Individuals, families, and faith communities have largely abdicated our concern over and care for the corpses of our dead.

What we do with our dead bodies will not save us from death on individual or planetary scales. But dead bodies hold ethically revelatory potential in a society of excessive individualism, consumerism, and ecological destruction. The corpse may very well be our ultimate challenge to Western notions of self-sufficiency and dominant narratives of human supremacy, standing over and above the web of life on earth. How we make sense of the corpse and act in relation to it can either reify culturally dominant discourses or help us deconstruct them.

Here, we take the corpse as our starting place of theological inquiry. The corpse is a site of human experience that can potentially help us make meaning and construct action in relation to our ecological, anthropological, relational, and technological entanglements and make important judgments about what constitutes health, harm, and practices of healing in relation to our dead bodies and our human enfolding within the larger web of life.

In our current milieu of the commodification of the corpse, the professionalization of deathcare, and the industrialization of the funeral, changes in deathcare are becoming increasingly market driven. A *theology* of the corpse, however, must transcend "the market as God" to ask more pressing questions about our collective life and death set within an ultimate context.[4] Whatever corpse care practices emerge in this era should not simply represent an expansion of consumer choice in a widening deathcare panoply.[5] We must consider interrogations of care for the dead as questions of vital significance to the living related to an assemblage of much larger ecological and social contexts into which our bodies—dead and alive—are integrally embedded.

A Theology of Dirt

The biblical writers had much to say about the "land." In fact, one way to narrate Israel's story is to acknowledge the movement from landlessness (wilderness, exile) to landedness (possession or anticipation of land or even grief over loss of land).[6] Admittedly, modern critical scholarship has tended to focus on "possession of land," a highly complicated and still contested notion—witness the current Palestinian-Israeli conflict. But possession of the land in the biblical tradition has always been tethered to Torah obedience, a fact not always recognized in the scholarly literature until fairly recently.[7] The writer of Deuteronomy made this point abundantly clear:

> If you obey the commandments of the Lord your God that I am commanding you today, by loving the Lord your God, walking in his ways, and observing his commandments, decrees, and ordinances, then you shall live and become numerous, and the Lord your God will bless you in the land that you are entering to possess. But if your heart turns away and you do not hear, but are led astray to bow down to other gods and serve them, I declare to you today that you shall perish; you shall not live long in the land that you are crossing the Jordan to enter and possess. I call heaven and earth to witness against you today that I have set before you life and death, blessings and curses.[8]

The connections between land possession and obedience to God, the "ultimate land owner," are conveniently and consistently forgotten by the military-industrial complex, intent on destroying opposition to its insatiable desire for more and more "territory" to the demise of all involved. This unbridled sense of land entitlement, whether on the part of ancient Israel or the colonial impulses of modern Western powers, is an insidious ideology that has commodified land into property and territory. Such land commodification has resulted in viewing the earth, on the one hand, as a property to be exploited by corporate agribusiness for profit in food production and, on the other hand, as a territory to be conquered, with the land's Indigenous populations exiled or extinguished. Torah obedience and the recognition that "the earth is the Lord's and all that is in it" provide a necessary, but all too often ignored, constraint.[9]

Furthermore, as important as was the theme of land possession in the Older Testament of Christian Scripture, early Christian writers showed a marked disinterest in the "land" as a visible sign of God's promises. Paul, for example, the earliest Christian writer who has left a literary legacy, is remarkably uninterested in a "theology of land" that entails conferring special recognition on a "Holy Land." This is most significant in his discussions of the Abrahamic promise, which in Paul's construal (and despite the significance of the "promised land" in its original iteration in Gen 12) pays essentially no attention to the role of the land in the promise to Abraham. For Paul, that promise is pan-ethnic and turns on the distinction between Abraham being justified by works (e.g., circumcision) or faith. Paul clearly favors the latter: "Abraham believed God, and it was reckoned to him as righteousness."[10] There is, of course, much debate regarding the specific claims Paul makes about Abraham and his faith, but the crucial point here is that the "promised land" plays no role. Likewise, other New Testament writers either ignore the question of Israel as a "Holy Land" or relativize it as a location among other "holy places."[11]

This is not to say, however, that the biblical writers, Old Testament and New Testament alike, had no interest in the earth or dirt, as it were. The Hebrew term *ereṣ*, after all, can refer to the ground, a political territory (and at times, specifically the land of Israel), or what contemporaries might label the planet earth.[12] It is the former agrarian sense of *ereṣ* as ground or dirt or fertile soil that underlies creation theology as a major motif in the Jewish Scriptures. This sense of land and the human vocation to care for it underlies the Genesis creation story(ies), a vocation that, in a tragic irony, has been masked in most English translations and used to warrant human superiority over—and misuse of—God's created order (e.g., in the NRSV of the Priestly account, humankind was to "have dominion over" every living thing; Gen 1:28). Equally problematic is the translation of the Yahwist account in Genesis 2:15, in which "God took the man and put him in the garden of Eden to till it and tend it" (NJPS). The English terms *till* and *tend* are horticultural and agricultural and are not, as Ellen Davis has argued, particularly apt renderings of the Hebrew *lĕʿobĕdāh ûlĕšomĕrāh*. Rather, Davis has argued provocatively and convincingly that the phrase might be more faithfully rendered as follows: "And YHWH God took the human and set him in the garden to work and serve it, to preserve and observe it." She comments further, "The human does not take priority over the land. Adam comes to Eden as a protector, answerable for the well-being of the precious thing he did not make; he is to be an observer, mindful of limits that are built into the created order as both inescapable and fitting. The biblical writer does not subscribe to the fantasy that our society has embraced as an ideal—that human ingenuity runs against physical limits only to overcome them. Rather . . . the land instantiates limits that God has set; we encounter it as a fellow creature to be respected and even revered."[13]

The apostle Paul also understood how intertwined the human creature is with the rest of the created order:

> For the creation waits with eager longing for the revealing of the children of God; for the creation was subjected to futility, not of its own will but by the will of the one who subjected it, in hope that the creation itself will be set free from its bondage to decay and will obtain the freedom of the glory of the children of God. We know that the whole creation has been groaning in labor pains until now; and not only the creation, but we ourselves, who have the first fruits of the Spirit, groan inwardly while we wait for adoption, the redemption of our bodies.[14]

Furthermore, Paul understood that this bodily redemption included the return of the body to the earth.[15]

Our most fundamental relationship, then, is with dirt—with "land" in its most material sense. And it is to that respected and revered dirt that our bodies return upon our death, at least in our theological imagination, if not always in our actual practice.

"Earth to Earth, Ashes to Ashes, Dust to Dust"

This liturgical phrase in funerary rites is indicative of the disposition of our bodies in the earth, as has been the typical Christian practice.[16] In Ecclesiastes 3:20, Qohelet, the teacher/author of the book, reflects on the fate shared by humans and animals alike in death, saying, "All are from the dust, and all turn to dust again." The word *dust* here is again the word used in Genesis 2:7, when God forms humanity from the dust of the ground. But even more critical in the Genesis text, the very word we use to describe "man" (*ha 'adam*)—where we get the proper name Adam for the first man—is tied inextricably to the earth itself. It is from the dust of the ground, *ha 'adamah*, that God forms the human, *ha 'adam*. We might literally think of Adam meaning something like earth creature, or dust creature, or mud creature.

Then in Genesis 2:9, the creation account continues with this description: "Out of the ground [*ha 'adamah*] the Lord God made to grow every tree that is pleasant to the sight and good for food." The very substance of the human is bound up in the account of primordial divine creativity with the earth itself, in the dust of the earth, and in common fate. So Qohelet says, "For the fate of humans and the fate of animals is the same; as one dies, so dies the other. They all have the same breath, and humans have no advantage over the animals; for all is vanity. All go to one place; all are from the dust, and all turn to dust again."[17] This verse contains a theological message that subverts ideologies of human supremacy bound up in our theologies and practices by drawing upon death itself as the clearest window into how we are intimately related to every other living creature—through our movement toward death, through our shared breath, through our emergence and return to earth, to humus, to dust.

We might hear in this text another iteration of Qohelet's realist appraisal of the human and the animal: *that our fates are bound up with one another*, not simply that we share the same fate of death. Qohelet invites movement beyond an ecological caretaking mode—one of humans over against "nature"—to help us see the human as a *mutual relational participant* in the larger web of life. This is part of an anthropological narrative that suggests an earthy entanglement, the human as integrally intertwined with other earth creatures. It summons an ethic of ecological solidarity, embracing our intimate relationality to the larger web of life. Key to Qohelet's portrayal of solidarity is the vision that this relational mutuality is forged through common precarity, ephemerality, even the fate of death and disaster: "For no one can anticipate the time of disaster. Like fish taken in a cruel net, and like birds caught in a snare, so mortals are snared at a time of calamity, when it suddenly falls upon them."[18]

This is not just the inevitability of death for the human and the animal but death and disaster on a larger scale: climate catastrophe, species extinction, ecosphere collapse. This ethic of ecological entanglement goes beyond protecting the earth out of a deep sense of appreciation or for the preservation of life's livability for future *human* generations. It pushes toward a perspective of relational mutuality in which the earth and its more-than-human inhabitants *desire things from us* and make *ethical demands* upon our lives. These demands and desires of the earth are not simply about us or our human livability or our happiness. They are about the good of other creatures, the web of life itself, formed from the *ha 'adamah*, sharing a mutual fate that is bound up with ours.

When any species is headed for disaster, it is *every species*, including the human, that is bound up in that fate of destruction. When any regional biosphere is threatened by climate calamity, *every creature* is drawn into the breath and soil of that place, not simply because we care about it on an emotional level, but because we are inextricably entangled in its well-being for its own sake, not just for ours. When we look appreciatively at the earth and every creature and landscape within it that we long to save for our progeny or enjoyment or human livability, the creatures and the soil itself look back at us with demands and desires of their own.

The land itself—the earth—is revelatory: earth speaks, earth desires, earth responds.

An Intimate Relationship with Dirt and Decay

It is more than the land as a broad concept that is important in an exploration of our body's relationship to the earth. We are bound up in an intimate relationship with *soil* more specifically. And yet we understand only a fragment of the relationship. Likely only about 1 percent of the microorganism species making up the soil's biological diversity have been identified, and its complex constitution is comprised of interactions of geological, biological, and social processes that are difficult if not impossible to disentangle.[19] We exist in an intimate relationship with soil, and this is a relationship of absence and grief if we are paying attention.

The earth has lost half of its topsoil in the last 150 years. This is largely due to the conversion of forests and grasslands into farmland for agriculture. Soil erosion increases the pollution of waterways, affects the livability of fish and other species, and creates worsening floods when degraded land can no longer hold onto water within the soil itself.[20] It is difficult to go a week or two without learning of a devastating flood in some part of the world, the severity of which is attributable to human-shaped changes to the environment and the climate.

We are indelibly and inextricably bound up with dirt. Robert Pogue Harrison calls this *the humic foundation of our life worlds.* "A humic foundation," he says, "is one whose contents have been buried so that they may be reclaimed by the future. The humic holds in its conserving element the unfinished story of what has come to pass."[21] Humans bury our dead not just to bring about a sense of closure in the loss of a beloved one but to "humanize the ground" on which we build our worlds and establish our histories.[22] We ritualize our relationship with the soil and with particular lands by placing the human within the humus, returning the *ha 'adam* to the *ha 'adamah.*

But as our relationship with land and soil erodes, our sense of relatedness between our bodies and the wider ecological web is ritualized differently. As practices of mastery increase, supported by theological and political narratives of dominion and domination, our sense of shared fate and intimate relationship with the soil morphs into a relationship of control over ecological processes, including the process of decay.

Our most common practices of body disposition in Western contexts involve either burial of a chemically embalmed body within a hardwood or metal casket and a cement or metal vault or grave liner or, alternatively, energy-intensive cremation by flame. Both contemporary conventional burial and flame cremation are technological practices of domination that subvert the potential of the body's return to the earth in any ecologically dynamic sense. Conventional embalming and burial attempt to subvert the process of decay and cut the body off from the surrounding earth with sealed caskets and vaults. Cremation removes the body's possibility of return to the earth through the reduction of the body to several pounds of remains that hold no nutrient properties.

As is evident from the previous chapters, we did not adopt these practices in order to simply subvert the body's return to the earth. There were historic trajectories and specific circumstances that gave rise to these practices. But they should not be perpetuated uncritically simply because they are the practices most dominant in today's North American deathcare landscape.

Perhaps seeing the horrors of decay on Civil War battlefields is a factor in our changed collective relationship with decay. It wasn't exactly "natural" in any sense to see that many decaying bodies, victims of horrifically violent deaths, in one place at one time. These battlefield devastations came at a time when industrial possibilities of deathcare were nascent and options that didn't exist before suddenly did. Entrepreneurial men saw a need to return bodies to families and developed the technological means of doing so. Embalming was a technological means of mastery over the corpse and over decay as the trajectory of the dead body. But it was developed in a context of extremity and trauma, and one unlike the context of most deaths prior to or after the Civil War. Yet the practices stuck in the imaginations of postbellum generations.

Embalming and burial within caskets and containers, increasingly sealed off from the surrounding earth, cemented a removed relationship from dirt and decay. "Earth to earth, ashes to ashes, dust to dust" became a macabre metaphor and no longer a material reality. And when we imagine our relationship with the larger earth of which we are a part, the visceral knowledge of one's eventual return to this enfolding web of life and death is absent. Our relationship with dirt and decay—intimate partners in life as in death—becomes increasingly severed.

Environmental geographer Jamie Lorimer argues that in the modern European imagination, "nature is green, not brown, and life is disconnected from aesthetics of death and decay."[23] Even in our engagement with "nature," we attempt to banish decay: looking upon green trees in a forest with an eye for their beauty and upon dead or dying trees with regret. All the while the dead trees—brown, not green—are full of life brought about by rot and decay, by *death.*

Lorimer relates a "profound lesson in finitude" first iterated to him by a botanist colleague as they ate apples together in a neglected urban cemetery: "She traced the fruit's possible molecular history—from subterranean human corpse, broken by bacteria, carried in the body of a worm to the reaching roots. Lifted high to branch, to bud, and finally to fruit. A bite, a chew, a swallow, and, after some acidic digestion, into me. From human to humus to human again through a humorous, rotten epiphany."[24] Such are the ways of the macrobiome and the larger life of decay: microbes and beetles and worms, carrion-eating creatures of the earth and sky, dead wood supporting abundant life-forms, mycelium threads beneath the soil's surface transporting nutrients through vast networks.

Carl Jung's psychological understanding of human thoughts and emotions was shaped by a perspective of a "universal soil" shared by humans and other forms of life. Jung portrayed humanity as increasingly isolated in the cosmos as we've become gradually cut off from emotional involvement in "nature," and our reciprocal relationships with earthy entities like trees, animals, mountains, stones, and plants have become flattened and objectified by scientific understanding, turning subjects into objects. This decreasing involvement with the surrounding ecological world has, in Jung's view, also diminished our emotional lives and the symbolic connection with that which once enlivened us.[25]

We are living and dying at a precarious point in the history of our human relationship with humus. While many projects are underway to help put humans back into dynamic relationship with the "universal soil" in which we are inextricably entangled with every form of life, it is the corpse—our own dead bodies—that holds the revelatory potential of decay. But only if we do not turn away from the profound lessons in finitude held in our own bodies—a "rotten epiphany" revealing the lively nature of our earth-entangled beingness. Turning away from the corpse only reifies our denial of decay and the wedge our deathcare practices now drive between our bodies and the larger web of life.

What Is a Corpse? A Dead-Body Theology

Feminist discourse over the past several decades provides a rich resource to draw upon when reflecting upon the "body."[26] Attempts by "second wave" feminists to reunite mind and body, split apart by Cartesian dualism ("I think, therefore I am"), were initially and largely successful in exposing the underlying assumptions of Western dualism: "The aim towards transcendence of our earthly conditions, so the argument goes, is, in fact, a thinly veiled desire to leave behind the fallen world of nature and women."[27] For feminists such as Gloria Steinem and Mary Daly, "the female body was a battleground. It was the site in which women were to regain control of that which had been taken from them by pornography, medicine, law and male sexual violence."[28] Feminist discourse levels a powerful critique at traditional Western thought that elevates the mind and spirit to the neglect of the body, but this discourse, understandably, focuses on the abuse and manipulation of *living* female bodies to the neglect of the corpse in that discussion.

More recent theological explorations of the "body," however, have moved from passive oversight to outright rejection of the corpse as a legitimate site of theological inquiry. Luke Timothy Johnson explores the body in a variety of relationships: the spirit and the body, the body at play, the body in pain, the passionate body, the body at work, the exceptional body, and the aging body.[29] But Johnson does not deal with the dead body. He defends this choice:

> But it is the living human body—individually and communally—that I take to be the arena or medium of the disclosure of the

> divine Spirit, the primary place where the Living God's work in creation finds expression, and thus the constantly shifting site that demands the theologian's constant attention. Body apart from spirit does not have the same theological interest. A dead human body, a corpse, can reveal all kinds of things to the trained observer; an autopsy can trace the past of the former human's existence in exquisite detail through the examination of dead organs and limbs. The dead body can give up the cause of its death; but lacking spirit, such a corpse cannot give the reasons why it lived. The pathologist and the criminologist should have the most intense interest in the body from which the human spirit has fled and which has become food for other living things. The theologian likewise should have the most intense interest in the ways the living body gives expression to spirit and thereby is a medium through which the Spirit of God is revealed.[30]

Likewise, Paul Griffiths also dismisses interest in the corpse because it is not what he labels "Christian flesh"; rather, Griffiths distinguishes between animate "flesh" and inanimate "body," and the corpse falls clearly into the latter category: "For mammalian flesh, to which human flesh belongs, the flesh-constituting gift exchange begins in the womb and ends only when death makes flesh into corpse. . . . Nonliving bodies neither caress nor wound and therefore don't give the distinctive fleshly gift of being able to do those things."[31] For Griffiths, the distinction between "flesh" and "body" turns on the "haptic" nature of flesh, the ability to touch and be touched (in either a caressing or wounding act). Griffiths concludes, "It's only when flesh cannot touch or be touched that it ceases to be flesh: then it is dead and has become body. . . . The only thing that prevents fleshly touch is death."[32]

But touch is not the only mode available to human flesh for "interacting with the world in which it finds itself." Seeing nonliving (human) flesh as something necessarily other than Christian flesh is a larger diminishing move toward its relationship to the other-than-human world. The turn away from the corpse in body theology has been premature and too restrictive. One should not dismiss too quickly the nonliving and its relation to the living, to the larger web of life, and to the theological tradition.

Exceptionalism or Entanglement?

Griffiths's theological depiction of the haptic nature of flesh—the ability to touch and be touched through a flesh-constituting gift exchange beginning in the womb and ending at death—is indicative of a narrative of human exceptionalism that limits our perspective on just what our bodies really are (alive *and* dead). Flesh-constituting gift exchanges do not end in death unless we intentionally prevent them. And the notion of "exchange" itself relies too heavily on a presumption of bounded individualism, as if our bodies are something we possess and can *volunteer* as a gift to others rather than containing multitudes of other-than-human life from the start. Both human exceptionalism and bounded individualism are narratives that pervade our contemporary deathcare practices and limit our theological perspectives on just what we're talking about when we talk about the corpse.

Human exceptionalism sets the human over against "nature" in a position of superiority or supremacy. The presumed exceptionalism and supremacy of humanity theologically hinge on the aforementioned faulty reading of Genesis 1, in which humanity is assumed to have "dominion" over the earth, sitting at the top of a universal and divinely ordained hierarchy of life. Bounded individualism presumes that we, as individual human beings, are entities unto ourselves—autonomous, self-contained, solely *human* human beings walled within our own skin.

The corpse considered within the wider web of life defies the rationality of human exceptionalism and bounded individualism. We are porous, complexly constituted, entangled with other beings. Being "co-constituted with the world, ontologically inseparable" is our very human condition.[33] It is from the dust of the ground, *ha 'adamah*, that God forms the human, *ha 'adam*. From humus to human to humus again. That is the theological cycle of the body.

We have for too long spoken of everything "not us" as if it were *less than us*, there for the taking, for extraction, for destruction, to use as "resources" to benefit us in the short term. This human supremacy and othering of the other-than-human has also been foundational for many of our practices of coloniality and racialized violence. For one example among so many, the philosopher Georg Hegel (1770–1831) wrote disparagingly about Africans in *The Philosophy of History*, saying they were "still involved in the conditions of mere nature."[34] This form of dehumanization, and the racial violence and colonization that results, is made thinkable by drawing upon the ideology of human supremacy *over against* "nature" and then *dehumanizing* some humans to the *status of* the natural, the wild and untamed as defined by Eurocentric culture or law or Christocentric religion. Women and LGBTQ people also experience the violence that results from a too-close relationship with "nature."

We are now being put in our place, not at the top of a great chain of being, but entangled in a vast web of creativity and creation currently on the brink of destruction. We can only imagine ourselves as outside of this cyclical web of entangled relations if we turn our gaze from the web of life, including multitudes living within. There is, after all, a microbiome at work within each of us, sustaining our life and the lives of multitudes that are as much a part of "our" bodies as anything else we consider a part of "us."

The term *microbiome* was coined by molecular biologist Joshua Lederberg, who used the term "to signify the ecological community of commensal, symbiotic, and pathogenic microorganisms that literally share our body space."[35] The human body is inhabited by bacteria that outnumber our human cells ten to one. To say that another way, your body is inhabited by ten times more nonhuman bacteria than it is *human* cells. (This calls into question just exactly where the boundaries of our presumed bounded individualism lie.) Our microbiome, residing in especially high numbers in our gastrointestinal tract, is a beneficial collection of bacteria necessary for life.

As Jane Bennett argues, "It is thus not enough to say that we are 'embodied.' We are, rather, *an array of bodies*, many different kinds of them in a nested set of microbiomes."[36] We can read the creation accounts of Genesis in this light. From the dust of the ground—out of the humus—God made the human. Through a divine piecing together of constituent parts from the larger web of life, humans came into being. And in the image of God—whose constituent parts span the cosmos—the divine crafted the human body and breathed into us *life*. In this light, theologian Sally McFague has helpfully described the earth as *God's body*.[37] But the earth is *our* body too. We are made from earthy multitudes and made up *by* them. We belong to the web of life.

As much as theologians have tried—and Griffiths's and Johnson's denial of the theological importance of the corpse is complicit in this attempt—we cannot at this critical stage of ecological crisis, climate collapse, and racialized violence continue to uphold human exceptionalism and bounded individualism with our theological renderings of the body. As Bruno Latour helpfully states, "There is no cure for the condition of belonging to the world. But, by taking care, we can cure ourselves of believing that we do not belong to it . . . that what happens to the world does not concern us."[38] We are not just in *relationship* to the larger web of life—even to the soil—we *belong* to it. We are composed of a humic tie from which we cannot extricate ourselves. A denial of the importance of the flesh in death is coterminous with our denigration of the earthy materiality of the web of life more broadly.

As witnessed in the previous chapters, we have done all that is humanly possible to prevent this porous, complex, coconstitutive entanglement by subverting the process of our bodies' return to the earth in death. (From dust to dust? Over our dead bodies!) There is a connection between our fear of decay and the ideologies of human exceptionalism and bounded individualism. If we—our bodies—break down, we are no longer individuals. Unaided by energy-intensive intervention, we return to something larger than us, more anonymous, more eco-cosmopolitan.

Yet having convinced ourselves of our place at the top of the food chain—not to mention the Great Chain of Being—we have a difficult time giving our flesh over to earth-others in death. The exchange of our molecules with those of the earth finally submits our ideologies (idolatries?) of supremacy to the truth that we are part of a web of life, and many members of that web are inextricably part of "us." The state of our bodies in death denies our exceptionalism and, quite literally, breaks down our notions of bounded individualism. Theologically, economically, and politically, we've long held a stake in preventing this truth from penetrating our lives—or our bodies.

Alexis Shotwell accurately names this posture of prevention a form of "defensive" and "possessive" individualism, arguing that "a species of defensive individualism" is one upholding "the sense in which the self is imagined as a fortress, separable from the world and requiring defense against the world."[39] Further, "possessive individualism is densely racialized; the core idea that our selves are owned by us functions as a categorical move to lay out a map of who can own others."[40] While our deathcare practices are not the pinnacle of our defensive and possessive forms of individualism, they do serve as a final—perhaps ultimate—reification of the values of exceptionalism, supremacy, and individualism that rend our perceived sense of connection with the wider web of life.[41] One way in which we must subvert this reification, especially within faith communities, is to resist the urge that Griffiths and Johnson so blithely bless by refusing to dismiss the dead body as an entity of theological importance.

A Death-Near Theology

Theologian John Boopalan argues that a Christian desire not to let death have the last word has led us to disallow death from having *any* word. This silencing of the corpse is even more potent when the dead bodies in question are produced through injustice and violence. Boopalan writes, "This is not simply a case of becoming wiser in hindsight. If the deaths of the past did not stop the world in its tracks, what about the present? Does news of death stop us in our tracks, or do we simply keep moving, hardened by indifference to the need for justice and peace? Despite the powerful chants of #NoJusticeNoPeace arising from the voices of those suffering violence, it seems that peace is often brokered at the cost of justice. Why? Is it possibly because of the tendency to theologize death away?" Boopalan then asks, "What if we treated death and suffering as having the last word? How would that change us and the world we live in?"[42]

A body-disparaging theology of death is a position of privilege. If our bodies mattered in life, they need not matter in death: "Just remember us how we were." Pay no attention to the portent of decay. Do not look upon the signs of an earthy claim upon our bodies. And if our bodies did not matter to the majority, to the powerful, to the structures and institutions of privilege's upholding in life, they are all too easily erased in death. That erasure must be refused by the communities to whom the body belongs as meaningful matter, even in death. We witness this refusal of the body's erasure in death in the forms of care practice in relation to bodies that were treated as if they did not matter in life. Even if we are not content to let death have "the last word," a death-near theology allows us to lean in close to learn what we can from the corpse without needing to defensively theologize death and the body away. This compassion toward the corpse may well help change us and the world we live in, as Boopalan hopes.

The Erasure of Indigenous Corpses

The prompting event of Boopalan's words was the discovery of 215 bodies of dead First Nations children on the grounds of a residential school in Kamloops, British Columbia, Canada.[43] Just a few days after his writing, another 761 bodies were found in unmarked graves on the site of a former residential school in Saskatchewan, Canada.[44] Cooperation between the Canadian government and ecclesial authorities led to the Catholic Church running about 70 percent of the schools, with Protestant denominations running most of the other 30 percent. Residential schools are also a significant part of the history of US violence against Native Americans. Today, the Canadian government is providing around 4.9 million Canadian dollars to Indigenous communities to search for more graves.

Indigenous communities in the United States and Canada actively refuse to let the bodies of their recent ancestors remain forgotten, erased by practices of coloniality. The residential schools were places where Indigenous young people were sent to have their own cultural heritages, knowledges, and languages stripped from them by the epistemic violence of indoctrination and assimilation into Eurocentric, Christocentric, white-normative ways of life. The high death toll at these schools is due to the overcrowded conditions, poor sanitation, inadequate food and health care, and practices of physical violence toward the children.[45]

This history of colonial violence continues to come to heinous fruition in the disturbingly high occurrence of missing and murdered Indigenous women and girls in our present context.[46] As Mvskoke geographer Laura Harjo describes it, *futurity* hinges on attending to the deaths of these Indigenous women and girls. Harjo writes, "This is different from a legacy. Futurity can mean that yet-to-be-conceived possibilities are invoked in us by the memory, energy, and personal narratives of these murdered and missing Indigenous women and girls."[47]

The erasure of Indigenous lives is bound up with violence perpetrated against Indigenous memory and Indigenous futurity. A recovery and reclamation and a commitment to provide care for the corpses of victims of residential schools are tied to an act of remembering and *re-membering*—putting back together again communities across time and space rent by colonial violence. Shotwell helpfully states, "It is key to hold in mind that the stakes of memory and forgetting are not equal;

white people, and white settlers in particular, benefit from forgetting the past that organizes the racist present, Indigenous people bear the weight of memory oppression."[48] Recovering the bodies of these Indigenous dead is an act of resistance to this long history of memory oppression. Shotwell continues, "Memory is held not only, or perhaps even not primarily, in our skull. Rather, it might be best understood as 'held' within precisely the complex network of relationships that shape affect and personhood."[49]

The bodies recovered from unmarked and forgotten graves are the material remains of the lives taken and memories erased. Even in their deaths, their future communities—those living now amid the discovery of their young bodies in the graves of the schools that tortured their living bodies—will not let their corpses go. Their future communities are reaching back toward these children in care for their bodily remains, claiming that they belong to a living community, even in death. And not only in acts of remembrance but in acts of caring re-membering of their dead bodies with the living communities that continue to claim them.

The Black Corpse on US Streets

Eighteen-year-old Michael Brown stood on the streets of his family's neighborhood in Ferguson, Missouri, hands raised in the air before being fatally shot six times by a Ferguson police officer. As his body lay on the sweltering August street in view of his friends and neighbors, Brown's grandmother came upon the scene looking for her grandson, who had been on his way to visit. In the gathering of family and friends and neighbors that grew on the street that day—before the three waves of protests that roiled through the following summer—something vitally important happened. Michael Brown's community stayed with his body.

Pastoral theologian Chanequa Walker-Barnes describes the impromptu vigil that developed on the streets of Ferguson that day: "Quietly, they watched as the coroner's office finally showed up at the scene. Then, when Michael's body had been loaded onto the coroner's van, they followed, walking en masse to the police department. There, too, they waited calmly for someone to come outside and explain why Brown had been shot when, as the word had already spread, his hands had been up."[50] Their somber poses, their insistence on staying with the body, their demands for accountability for Brown's killing, Walker-Barnes says, were "a historic African American mourning ritual."[51] Through their actions, their closeness to Brown's body even in death, his community responded to what Karla Holloway identifies as the central question of African American mourning: "Who's got the body?"[52]

The police, however, took their presence, their insistence on staying with his body, and their calls for accountability and information as a threat and responded with militarized force and a curfew. The national reckoning that surrounded Brown's killing by police in Ferguson was historic. But it was Brown's dead body that became the site of mourning and lament and a striving toward accountability for justice. It was his body that the crowd followed that day before the streets of Ferguson were filled with protestors from all over the country. His community followed him, as in funeral processions of old, through the streets of the city as he traveled in a coroner's van to the morgue. Brown's community stayed with his body. They insisted that his body mattered, even in death.

The connection between the corpses of Black bodies killed through acts of violence and a community of mourning, lament, and striving toward justice has a lengthy history. We might recall the tenacity of Mamie Till Mobley, who, when she saw the body of her son Emmett Till after he had been murdered and mutilated and thrown into the Tallahatchie River in an act of racist violence, insisted that the country look upon his corpse. The funeral directors strongly recommended to her a closed-casket funeral. But Mamie Till Mobley refused and insisted the casket be open and photographs taken, saying, "Let the people see what they did to my boy."[53]

In a refusal to look away from the bodies of their dead or to have those bodies too quickly taken from their accompaniment, the community of Michael Brown and the mother of Emmett Till and many other African American communities have stayed with the bodies of their beloved ones taken in acts of violence and insisted that the country *see* not just injustice and violence in the abstract but the *bodies* of the dead.

The Collective for Radical Death Studies (CRDS) continues this work in the scholarly arena of death studies. The CRDS describes itself as a collective of scholars, funeral directors, death work practitioners, activists, and students "who view death work as synonymous with antiracism work, synonymous with actively dismantling oppression, and as a way to validate cultural and social life among marginalized groups" with the aim of "decolonizing death studies in theory and in practice."[54] And death work's connection with antiracism and the dismantling of oppression insists that we must sit with our dead long enough to learn the lessons we each hold in our bodies, especially after death.

The Transgressive HIV/AIDS Corpse

Perhaps no collective in history is more practiced in sitting with the bodies of the dying and dead than LGBTQ communities across the United States during the height of the HIV/AIDS epidemic in the late 1980s and early 1990s. Many medical professionals treated the body infected with HIV/AIDS as a pariah when they were alive, and many funeral directors outright refused to accept a body that died of HIV/AIDS. Some charged exorbitant prices to care for the bodies of AIDS victims. Other funeral directors portrayed their work with the HIV/AIDS dead as the work of heroes, describing in detail the supposedly herculean task of caring for the bodies.

Funeral directors and embalmers also experienced a rupture in their own carefully spun narrative of deathcare. They no longer trusted their own practices, heralded as technologies to make the dead body sanitary and presentable to the public. The corpses of those who died with HIV/AIDS sent ripples of doubt through the industry that were addressed in numerous publications attempting to reinforce the resolve of funeral directors and to hold embalming as the cornerstone of the profession. As John Erik Troyer argues, "The emergence of the HIV/AIDS corpse significantly destabilized notions of universal death, i.e., that *in death* American dead bodies were mostly the same. In fact, the American HIV/AIDS corpse was made doubly problematic by its exotic 'Otherness,' which was explicitly local and domestic."[55]

The disruption of the "normal" dead body produced rules and regulations aimed to inform deathcare practices with the HIV/AIDS corpse in order to "institutionalize extreme forms of homogeneity."[56] In part, the HIV/AIDS corpse brought about the 1991 US Department of Labor and the Occupational Safety and Health Administration's uniform federal rules for handling all dead bodies, or "universal precautions." The funeral industry now treated every corpse as if it were a potential biohazard.[57] These precautions have remained relatively stable ever since, applied to every corpse that enters the confines of the embalming room. But outside of funeral establishments, the bodies of people who died of AIDS took on a life of their own.

Early AIDS activists made the bodies of the dead "useful corpses," a claim Lauren DeLand makes specifically about the role of the AIDS corpse in the art of David Wojnarowicz, who "refashioned this vilified corpse into a political weapon to be detonated at the door of those directly responsible for perpetuating the epidemic."[58] The activist organization ACT UP (AIDS Coalition to Unleash Power) politicized funerals for those who died of AIDS, carrying coffins through the streets of New York City or ceremoniously placing the cremated remains of someone recently dead at the site of an organization culpable for the perpetuation of the epidemic. In 1992, the ashes of several people who died of AIDS were scattered on the White House lawn in an act of protest, the cremated remains thrown in plastic bags over the fence by their loved ones. DeLand writes of these acts in relation to the HIV/AIDS corpse, "So palpable is the sensation that the bereaved are doing something that they believe they must and yet obviously do not want to do."[59]

Troyer describes the HIV/AIDS corpse as a "queer corpse." Not necessarily or primarily an *LGBTQ corpse* but instead "a specific kind of dead body that has radically reworked the social and political dynamics of death and dying by challenging the transformative power of the technologies of the corpse that redefine the dead self."[60] The bodies of those who died of HIV/AIDS in the 1980s and 1990s upended a century and a half of technological control of the corpse by the funeral industry, calling well-established practices into question among those who depended on technologies like embalming to control the bodies of the dead.[61]

Legal scholar Ellen Stroud explains the confusion our cultural relations to the corpse cause when it comes to deciding what exactly the dead body *is* and *to whom* it belongs, saying, "And this is the central puzzle of the law of the dead: The human corpse is a thing, a material object—a messy, maybe dangerous, perhaps valuable, often useful, and always tangible thing—and the law has much to say about such things. But the dead human body is also something very different: It is also my father, and my friend, perhaps my child, and some day, me. For even the most secular among us, a dead human body is at the least a very peculiar and particular kind of thing."[62] She continues, "The corpses of the most vulnerable will always be the ones treated most like things."[63]

The HIV/AIDS-infected body in life and in death was, indeed, treated like a "thing," and a dangerous thing at that—to be kept at a distance, refused into the company of the living, vilified in life and in death. What is often missing from assessments of the HIV/AIDS corpse is the care given to the bodies of men dying with HIV/AIDS by members of their own community. Throughout the course of illness, in the moments leading to death, those dying of HIV/AIDS were often accompanied by partners, intimate friendship networks, and even strangers who volunteered to be paired with someone experiencing the effects of the disease by organizations like the Gay Men's Health Crisis.[64] In particular, lesbians stood with gay men dying of HIV/AIDS in care and solidarity throughout the early crisis year of the epidemic.

There were also some outside of LGBTQ communities like Ruth Coker Burks who defied the norms of the medical and funerary professions that desperately tried to avoid caring for those dying of HIV/AIDS. Burks provided the physical care and emotional support so desperately lacking for many in her care whose families had abandoned them when their diagnosis became known. She served as a caretaker for over one thousand families. And in their deaths, Burks became an advocate for them with her local funeral directors in Arkansas, served as a death doula for those needing care through their process of dying, and even buried many men who died of AIDS in her own family's cemetery.[65]

Informal networks of LGBTQ people, grassroots organizations like ACT UP and Gay Men's Health Crisis, and even lone individuals like Ruth Coker Burks refused to submit to a deathcare regime that marginalized the HIV/AIDS corpse. And just as importantly, the HIV/AIDS corpse itself—a queer corpse with transgressive potentiality—defied the well-established practices of the funeral profession and its presumed control over the dead. It became an *insistent* corpse that called together new forms of community to surround the bodies of the HIV/AIDS dead.

Conclusion

New questions arise over the course of time at the intersection between the living community and the bodies of the dead, giving rise to the adoption of new deathcare practices. Many of the hinge points in our changing relationship to the corpse traced in the previous chapters map onto the same sociopolitical narrative turns that have brought us to the brink of climate collapse and ecological degradation: colonialism and its extractive logic, population booms, industrialization, the emergence of a capitalist economic system, rampant consumption, disposability culture, and a religious abdication of concern for earthy materiality coupled with a zeal for the spirit and the otherworldly. Bodies—even corpses—act as signifiers of moral, economic, and political systems.[66]

The corpse matters to the wider web of life. But the corpse also matters to human communities, though we have developed a persistent denial of the corpse's relevance to the living. A theology that engages the corpse must sit with the body after death. A theology of the corpse must help us resist the urge to move on too quickly to a disembodied life of the soul or spirit. A death-near theology constructs the theological life of the faithful with and in relation to the corpse. We must sit with our dead long enough to learn the lessons we each hold in our bodies, especially after death.

4

The Corpse to Come

Imagining Deathcare Anew

What we do with and in relation to our dead in the twenty-first-century United States would look shockingly strange to our relatives of just a few centuries ago. Many of our deathcare practices would seem incomprehensible to most of our ancestors in human history before that. Understanding the genealogy of our relationship with the bodies of the dead should, if anything, open us to the possibility of relating to the dead differently in the near future, knowing that what we do with and to our dead at present are *not* rituals handed down through time immemorial. Instead, these rituals and practices took shape over time in response to the questions and concerns emerging in the context out of which they developed.

For faith communities, concerns of rituals and deathcare are especially important questions. New deathcare practices have typically come under the scrutinizing gaze of ecclesial authorities. But largely it seems that churches have now gotten out of the business of circumscribing people's deathcare choices. Perhaps inadvertently, churches have also gotten out of the ministry of deathcare altogether. It is time for churches to care about our deathcare choices again. What is done with our corpses is a theological concern with implications for how we see ourselves as human beings within a context of belongingness to the rest of the planet.

Here we will take a few of the emerging practices of deathcare that are becoming of more and more interest to those in North America and examine them theologically, looking at how each practice is shaped by ecological, anthropological, and technological ways of arranging relationships in the world and asking what possibilities each practice holds for health, harm, and healing for a people and a planet on the brink.

Emerging Practices of Corpse Care

The flaws and drawbacks of contemporary conventional American corpse care are described in detail in chapter 2. Yet there are also emerging practices challenging the predictability of this professionalized chain of events that are harder to squeeze into the status quo of deathcare in the United States. Having convinced ourselves of our place at the top of the food chain—as well as the Great Chain of Being—by defining our "humanity" over against the beingness of "nature," we have a difficult time giving our flesh over to earth-others in death. But we have never belonged to ourselves alone. We exist only in a complex web of interconnective mutuality, of ecological assemblages, of sympoiesis—worlds of *making-with* in the company of many others.[1]

Our ecologically entangled relationship with the wider web of life is one of the primary reasons for emerging deathcare choices that deviate from conventional modern burial and flame cremation. While the ecological concerns are important enough on their own, there are also larger theological concerns that arise in our relationship with the dead and with our own dead bodies, as we pointed to in the previous chapter.

Natural Burial (a.k.a. Green Burial)

Natural burial, or green burial, is what many of our ancestors practiced for generation upon generation. It is simply the practice of returning the body to the earth in a way that does not subvert the process of decay and the body's return to the surrounding web of life. This style of burial emerged, or *reemerged*, in Great Britain in the early 1990s—often called woodland burial there—and has spread throughout that country as well as through Canada.[2] The natural burial movement in the United States began much earlier with an idea to contribute to chestnut restoration through the act of conservation burial. The idea was conceived by a college student in the 1970s named Billy Campbell, who, after becoming a family physician in South Carolina, published the notion in a 1988 issue of an Appalachian bioregional journal called *Katúah*. There, Campbell remarked, "I wish my body to nourish a part of the living forest, marked only by a colony of trilliums or a chestnut tree, in an area that would be pleasant and rejuvenating for others to visit, in which they would be reminded of life's continuing cycles of growth and death, decomposition and rebirth. This would truly be a sacred place."[3]

The notion of conservation burial came to fruition in Westminster, South Carolina, with the 1996 founding of Ramsey Creek Preserve by Billy Campbell and his wife, Kimberley. Ramsey Creek was the first green cemetery in the United States and was "formed to harness the funeral industry for land protection and restoration, to fund non-profits, education, the arts and scientific research, and to provide a less expensive and more meaningful burial option."[4]

The Green Burial Council (GBC) certifies three levels of cemeteries practicing some form of natural burial: hybrid cemeteries, natural burial grounds, and conservation burial grounds. In all three levels of certification, the bodies buried are not embalmed (or, if so, only with GBC-approved, nontoxic chemicals), burial containers or shrouds are made of biodegradable materials, no vault or burial liner is used, and there is a provision for families to have some hand in the burial and ritual process at the grave. Typically, graves are not adorned with large, permanent stones or monuments.

In hybrid cemeteries, these provisions are usually met by practicing natural burial in a designated space within a cemetery where modern conventional burials are also taking place on other parts of the property. In natural burial grounds, the standards are elevated through an ecological impact assessment and special care given to ecologically sensitive areas in the burial ground. There is also a limitation on types and sizes of memorial markers (so that if they are used, they don't impair ecological conditions or the natural aesthetic of the grounds) as well as limitations on burial density within the grounds. When nonpermanent markers are used, or no markers at all, graves are usually GPS located and easily found using the burial ground's computer system. In many, if not most, conservation burial grounds, small, unobtrusive, engraved markers made from local stone can be placed atop the grave.

For conservation burial grounds—the most extensive level of certification—there are additional provisions, such as the application of strategies to conserve, preserve, enhance, or restore historic native or natural habitats and flora in the region; the conservation of a minimum of twenty acres (or five acres if contiguous to other protected land); operation in conjunction with a government agency or nonprofit conservation organization with a legally binding responsibility for perpetual monitoring of the easement; and a legally binding and irrevocable agreement that guarantees the preservation of the burial ground.[5] At the conservation level, the explicit purpose of placing bodies within a particular tract of land is to protect the land from harm and development or to restore the land from damage previously done. It is, in this sense, an ecologically activist form of burial. By 2019, about half of all US states had a natural burial ground or a section for natural burial within a conventional cemetery, and in 2021, there were around 353, with many others in the works (notably, only seven of these are conservation burying grounds).[6]

Robert Pogue Harrison argues that the surest way to take possession of a place is to bury one's dead in it.[7] But there are alternative ways of considering burial outside of narratives of possession and ownership. The natural burial movement exemplifies some of these alternative values. In natural burial, the body is seen as an integral participant in the larger web of life, and its materiality in death is a gift to the ecosphere that nurtured and sustained it in life. This is more akin to how other cultures have marked the earth with the graves of ancestors. Native Americans, for example, are carefully attuned to the ancestral presence in the landscapes inhabited by the living, and in no small part because these lands contain the bones of their dead. There is a *belongingness* to the land. "There is a difference," Harrison notes, "between proprietary claims and the claims of belonging, this despite the fact that in Western culture these two claims have a way of blending into each other."[8]

What is required now in Western capitalist societies is a radical reorientation of our sense of what we are doing when we put our bodies in the ground. This reorientation must resist the American way of property and ownership: claiming a plot of land for our own in perpetuity, with our dead bodies in secure vaults underground, topped by personalized headstones that say in so many words, "The earth belongs to us." Instead, we can place our bodies in the ground—into the earth—without the accouterments of industrialized deathcare in order to claim, "Our bodies belong to the earth." Dust to dust. From humus to human to humus again. A return home for the materiality of our bodies.

It is now common to hear arguments against conventional cemetery burial that go something like this: Land is precious and in short supply, so we desire not to take up any space that is unnecessary for us to occupy in death. This has long been an argument made by proponents of cremation, in fact. In conservation burial, however, the ethos of the movement is quite similar but with a radically different praxis of disposition. It goes something more like this: Land is precious, so we use our bodies to claim the space for the preservation and perpetual good of the land itself. And payment for our grave contributes to the care of that landscape so that it is free from the prospect of development and damage. In natural burial, our bodies—even in death—can work for the good of the ecological whole.

Race and the Green Burial Movement

It is observable in green burial seminars, conferences, and gatherings that the movement and its prominent figures are currently overwhelmingly white. This is a topic of interest and concern within green burial circles, as commitments to justice beyond the ecological and economic are close to the hearts of many green burial advocates. There is an opportunity for the green burial movement and congregations with an interest in natural burial to interrogate the racial dimensions of deathcare beyond current concerns of inclusivity. As we noted in the first two chapters, our deathcare practices have a long and close relationship to race.

Ownership of the land for one's burial plot became an expression of some degree of *freedom* in a Jim Crow era when land ownership was often denied to many African Americans. The simplicity of many modern natural burials, along with the propensity not to mark graves with anything more than a small stone that will one day likely be absorbed by the landscape, is a marked departure from a tradition of African American funerals that have honored the dead with extravagant displays of mourning and celebrating a lost loved one.[9] If we expand the scope of memory to include cultural memory of the distant past, simple burials with unmarked graves can bear an unintended resemblance to a history of African Americans buried at the edges of white burial grounds in graves unmarked or marked only by temporary markers that would eventually deteriorate and disappear as nearby white families were memorialized in perpetuity.

Yet there is also a way in which African American deathcare practices can be viewed as precursors to the modern natural burial movement if we look at the story of deathcare in the United States not as a linear narrative of evolution or progress but as cyclical or episodic. For example, the African American Mount Auburn Cemetery of Baltimore, discussed in chapter 2, is a historic site that exemplifies some of the commitments of the contemporary natural burial movement. Landscape architect Diane Jones argues that the Euro-American design of early rural cemeteries serves to deny the fact that these are places for the dead. Through formalized layouts, parklike atmospheres, "controlled planting and topography, aesthetic treatment, and grand monuments," these cemeteries made certain breaks with the natural landscape of the place.[10]

In contrast, Mount Auburn Cemetery of Baltimore maintained an overgrown look with a naturalistic appearance full of native and invasive plant species. In part, this is attributed to the lack of perpetual care and the personal responsibility of individuals and families for the upkeep of plots. But even more, this aesthetic is due to "the attitude toward nature, the land, and environment that is particular to African American culture." Jones continues, "Once overlaid by African-American culture, the cemetery becomes 'uncontrolled' as exemplified by Mount Auburn in Baltimore. Cemeteries in which African-Americans were buried often had grave depressions and mounded graves that signified the resting place of the dead. Grass growing over graves is not of great importance, and the use of specimen or symbolic planting is not often employed. Simplicity in planting and design is the common element in these cemeteries, with formalized planting often seen as an intrusion that would disturb the dead and the grave itself."[11]

Many of the commitments in African American burials exemplified in Baltimore's Mount Auburn Cemetery—temporary markers, burial mounds over the graves, simple plantings in the cemetery, and so on—are important historic precursors to the ideals of natural burial today. Importantly, these didn't emerge from the "green burial movement" as we've come to know it—a movement noticeably led by white individuals and institutions. Rather, many of the commitments of the movement are deeply rooted in the cultural traditions and religious expressions of African Americans. Our histories of the movement and imaginations of its future should recognize these points of connection along with their relationship to our larger history of race, colonization, and ecological domination.

As theologian Norman Wirzba notes, "From the outset, slavery went absolutely hand in hand with the reckless plundering of ecosystems in the New World."[12] The social context in which we enter discussions about our deathcare practices is a world shaped by these colonizing and extractive logics that separate human communities from their ecological homes in various ways and differently according to racial embodiment. For those shaped by the colonial ideologies of our European forebearers, extractive logics and ecological domination have made their way even into our graves, where what we extract from the earth in the form of carbon, metals, hardwoods, and so on ironically go back with us into the ground in energy-intensive forms of modern conventional burial. And as Achille Mbembe reminds us, "Extraction was first and foremost the tearing or separation of human beings from their origins and birthplaces."[13] Theologian Barbara Holmes draws out the implications of this extractive logic for many African Americans, saying, "As black folks toiled in cotton fields that they did not own and ran through swamps to escape slave-hunting dogs, they lost their ability to relate to the natural world as an intrinsic element of an inspirited community."[14] Our conversations, deliberations, and educational efforts on behalf of green burial should help us reckon with much larger questions of racial and ecological relationships that rest just beneath the surface of these grave considerations.

In its continued growth and advocacy, the green burial movement and all interested in the perpetuation of natural burial must attend to the practice of natural burial not only as an expression of environmental concern—which it certainly is—but also as a way of expressing diverse commitments that resist a history of colonial violence, capitalistic attachments to property and ownership, and ecological devastation in the name of "progress." In embodying these commitments in death, we all have much to learn from the deathcare practices of myriad others, from African Americans to Native Americans and, of course, from our Muslim and Jewish neighbors, for whom "natural burial" is simply "burial."

Trace Memorialization

In natural burial—especially at the conservation level—concerns of memorialization become important for many. The ideal of natural burial is to make as little of a human mark on the landscape as possible, returning the body to the earth in a way that is congruent with the earth's processes of reclaiming the materiality of the dead in transformation toward the materiality of life. But even for the strictest conservation burial grounds, it is a hard sell for many families to leave the grave of a loved one completely unmarked. In places like Ramsey Creek, small natural fieldstones can be engraved with the name of the deceased, dates of birth and death, or other small messages and placed upon the burial mound. After several years, however, these stones are often reclaimed into the earth as the flora of the forest grows up over the grave and the burial mound gradually levels off throughout the process of bodily decay.

Of course, if a continued relationship with the site of interment is desired, loved ones can visit and sit or walk among the shade of the trees in the deep woods of the conservation burial ground. If periodic gifts are desired in memory of loved ones, rather than flowers or grave goods left on a tombstone, financial donations can be made to the funds that contribute to the upkeep of the conservation area, just as a loved one's physical body is participating in the very life of that landscape and its vitality.

But the question of memorialization is still a pressing one for many. While conventional cemeteries are marked by a multitude of stone or metal monuments with epitaphs for the dead buried there, natural burial should not be viewed as devoid of memorialization practices. But what is left behind at the site of a natural burial—especially a conservation burial—are trace memorials: mounds atop bodies recently buried; coverings of branches, pine needles, or other flora of the landscape; and small stones that may enter the earth again in some years. Not memorials to human individuality in perpetuity but traces of human remains that remain in the landscape and are held by the earth.

Adam Searle draws upon the notion of the "trace" in the work of Jacques Derrida, explaining, "Thinking through traces is an act of foregrounding that which is absent, the being-there of the not-there. . . . Trace is not only that which is inferred from its nonpresence but also a deliberate reference to the marking of tracks, to the material and inerasable imprinting of action and event upon material medium."[15] Walking through a conservation burial ground like Ramsey Creek is walking among the traces—the being-there of the not-there—bodies returning to the earth beneath one's feet, under the trees, beside streams. Searle says, "These absences are immediate and fleeting engagements of the future as well as the past, both of which we may awkwardly encounter through the ways we act in the present."[16]

Memories of our individuality are present but fleeting. Traces mark a returning of human to humus alongside a cultural turning from our attachments to perpetual memorialization toward a memory that becomes palpable in the becoming of the body alongside the beings of the web of life surrounding and subsuming it.

Archaeologist and anthropologist of modern American deathcare Shannon Lee Dowdy writes, "I recently learned that scientists have discovered that most of the earth's forests have as much life belowground as above, much of it consisting of a tiny white fungal neural network that connects the entire system. I am not sure why this fact captivates me so much, but I am starting to think that this is how we should imagine relations between the past and the present, between the living and the dead."[17]

Thinking through traces, one can experience in the woodlands and prairies of natural burial grounds the present-absence of loved ones interred there in a tendril-like network of memory reaching from the present into the past and future of the very land in which a body is contained. Relationships of the living and the dead and the yet to live, human and other-than-human, are entangled in the traces of natural burial landscapes. In this type of trace memorialization, we subvert the urge toward human dominance of the land, even in death, and we give our bodies to the fleeting entanglements of past, present, and future in the web of life.

Three Religiously Founded Examples

In addition to the larger history and philosophy of the green burial movement, what is of particular interest to us here are the ways that Christian religious communities have engaged in the proliferation of natural burial in the United States. Three such examples are highlighted here due to the diversity of religious traditions they represent.

Honey Creek Woodlands in Conyers, Georgia, just outside of Atlanta, is a conservation burial ground started by the Trappist brothers at the Monastery of the Holy Spirit.[18] The monastery owns 2,300 acres of primarily woodland adjacent to 40,000 acres of the Arabia Mountain National Heritage Area. Though owned by a monastery, burial is not limited to Catholics at Honey Creek. While some choose burial there for religious reasons, others do so for environmental reasons, and still others for concerns of cost. Honey Creek advertises the prices of plots on their website, noting that "natural burial is generally about half the cost of a modern burial."[19] While no permanently affixed tombstones are allowed at Honey Creek, or most any conservation burial ground, the Woodlands does offer a small natural stone from the local area that can be engraved and placed atop the grave.

Heritage Acres Memorial Sanctuary started through the efforts of Heritage Universalist Unitarian Church in Cincinnati, Ohio. Environmental stewardship is the central commitment of Heritage Acres in "creating a nature preserve where people may be laid to rest naturally," expressing "compassion for both the earth, and . . . fellow human beings."[20] (Notably, at Heritage Acres, burial rights for pets can also be purchased.[21]) The senior minister of Heritage Universalist Unitarian Church, Bill Gupton, describes the process of finding the land for the burial ground, noting that one of the intangible requirements was that it needed to be land in need of saving, likely to become a development or a subdivision in the near future. Thus, Heritage Acres was begun as a place where both the people buried there and the landscape itself could coexist, conserving a piece of at-risk land as a nature preserve—an "open meadow filled with grass and wildflowers, surrounded by forest," with burials taking place in the prairie.[22]

Grace Church, an evangelical church in the Upstate of South Carolina, purchased 12.1 acres in the vicinity of the church's multiple campuses for a "natural burial ministry."[23] Three purposes animate the mission of Grace Church's natural burial ministry: to reclaim the church's role in deathcare while recentering the family in the process of body care and burial, to address the financial burden that conventional funerals place on many families, and to practice environmental stewardship through conservation.[24] Notably, however, burial at the church's natural burial ground is for church members and their families only and *not* for anyone in the wider community wishing to be buried there. And unlike Honey Creek and Heritage Acres, which inter many cremated remains alongside whole-body natural burials, Grace Church *only* provides for "a resting place in the ground for a recently deceased body," not for cremated remains.[25]

We name these three natural burial grounds among the many that exist in the United States because Honey Creek, Heritage Acres, and Grace Church's natural burial ministries were each founded by religious communities holding theological commitments that were parallel to those of the wider green burial movement. Religious communities have long undertaken large-scale projects that benefit their communities, from the founding of hospitals and halfway houses, to homeless shelters and food programs, to universities and disaster relief agencies. Communities of faith know how to do extraordinary things in community. For churches holding commitments of care for people across the life span (including death), wishing to honor a sense of communal grief, and desiring to embody environmental, economic, and other concerns of justice and care, the fields are ripe for harvesting.[26] And our bodies are the seeds.

Alkaline Hydrolysis (a.k.a. Water Cremation)

Many cities in the United States—along with many countries in the world—lack available land for burial and have increasingly turned to cremation as the preferred method of body disposition. In Nevada, the cremation rate in 2019 was 80.7 percent, with Oregon, Washington, and Maine not far behind. Mississippi is the state with the lowest cremation rate, at just 27.9 percent.[27] While cremation is a less expensive alternative to modern conventional burial and keeps hardwoods, metals, cement, and chemicals out of the ground (though many hardwood caskets are cremated and many cremated bodies are embalmed for viewing prior to cremation), there is an extensive carbon footprint for cremation, making it far less than ideal for those wishing to return their bodies to the earth in ecologically responsible ways.

Alkaline hydrolysis, also known as water cremation or aquamation, on the other hand, uses significantly less energy than flame cremation. The process uses a water, heat, and alkali-based solution instead of flames to speed the process of decomposition, returning the body to an ash-like powder that retains its nutrient properties. (Though the remains are not readily usable as fertilizer in any direct sense.) One study suggests not only that the net environmental impact of alkaline hydrolysis is less than that of conventional modern burials and flame cremation but that the recycling of metal from implants could fully offset alkaline hydrolysis's contributions to climate change.[28] Additionally, unlike flame cremation, alkaline hydrolysis relies on electricity as a source of energy, making the process more easily powered by renewable energies like wind, water, and solar as electric grids become more reliant upon renewable sources. And while not as energy intensive as flame cremation, alkaline hydrolysis does use intensive amounts of water, which is important to note in an age of increasing drought in many parts of the country.

In theologically and ethically assessing the use of alkaline hydrolysis as a method of disposition, technology becomes a key factor. Professor of religion and environmental studies at Swarthmore College Mark I. Wallace draws upon the distinction made by Martin Heidegger between *physis* and *techne* in ways that are helpful in this deliberation. The Greek word *physis*, for Heidegger, indicates a type of bringing-forth that involves growing the things that are already of the other-than-human natural world, while *techne* points to human intervention in transformational processes.[29] *Techne*, one of the Greek roots of *technology*, is a crafting activity, a form of making, and for Heidegger, it indicates forms of poetic creativity (*poiesis*).

Wallace explains, "Nothing, in other words, simply *is* because whatever *is* is always in the process of changing or being changed into something else—whether that process is naturally occurring (*physis*) or catalyzed by human creativity (*techne*)."[30] The question we must ask is whether our technological interventions into the process of deathcare and decay move *with* the *physis* of the earth or *against* it. Wallace again comments, "Is our practice of *techne*—or technology—thoughtfully attendant to the emerging patterns of relationship that naturally reoccur in the process of *poiesis* or bringing forth? Or is our technological intervention into nature's emerging process a violent 'setting-upon' that process . . . that pays little if any attention to the destructive impacts generated by our intrusions into the more-than-human world?"[31]

What should, by now, be clear is that technological interventions of embalming and conventional burial in vaults and grave liners alongside the technological advances of modern flame cremation work *against* the processes of the wider web of life in relation to the human corpse. These technologies subvert the desires of the earth in relation to the dead body by either cutting off access through burial in sealed caskets and vaults or burning the body through an energy-intensive, fossil-fuel-dependent process.

Alkaline hydrolysis, on the other hand, results in the reduction of the body to pulverized ash-like remains. However, the method by which it does so is far less energy intensive than flame cremation and results in remains that can still be nutrient rich when scattered or buried in a landscape. While permitted in twenty US states, alkaline hydrolysis is available in fewer than half of those states due to the cost to funeral homes of acquiring the technology and, presumably, uncertainty about the demand. Additionally, while the Cremation Association of North America deems alkaline hydrolysis a form of cremation, the National Funeral Directors Association does not, and casket producers actively lobby against the legalization of water cremation, as it would cut into their ability to sell caskets that can be buried or burned but are of no use in the process of alkaline hydrolysis.[32]

What is of even more interest here, however, is the opposition of the Catholic Church to water cremation. While the Catholic Church approves of flame cremation, it requires that the resulting remains be kept intact and deposited in a sacred space, like a cemetery. Ashes cannot be scattered, nor can they be kept in an urn in a loved one's home.[33] When alkaline hydrolysis was approved by the Wisconsin State Senate in May 2021, all five Catholic bishops in the state opposed the bill. Auxiliary Bishop James T. Schuerman stated, "Human beings are created in the image and likeness of God, and the human body, which reflects God's image in a special way, is sacred. When we bury or entomb human remains, we are honoring the body's sacredness. . . . Alkaline hydrolysis is a process of disposing of human remains, treating them like waste. The body is broken down in water and chemicals, and the liquid remains are disposed of in the wastewater system. This process does not show respect or reverence for the human body and stands in opposition to our Christian understanding of honoring the dead."[34]

The main sticking point for Catholic bishops seems to be the liquid remains of the process being deposited in drains that go into municipal wastewater systems. The unaccounted-for contradiction in this position, however, is that the liquid remains from the process of embalming—blood and other bodily fluids removed before the insertion of embalming fluid—also wash down the drain into wastewater systems. Yet embalming bodies remains an acceptable Catholic practice.

In further opposition to the flameless cremation bill, Wisconsin Catholic Conference director Kim Vercauteren argued, "The human body is a physical, material manifestation of God's image and shares in that dignity. Even in death, we show reverence and compassion for God's creation by praying for and laying to rest the departed."[35] Yet the position of the bishops and the Catholic Conference does not account for the environmental impact of conventional modern burials or flame cremation in the reverence and compassion shown for God's creation as explicated in Pope Francis's encyclical on the environment, *Laudato si'*.

Catholic communities will have to engage in substantive theological deliberation to reconcile divergences and seeming contradictions in church instruction on deathcare praxis. But other faith communities, too, have the opportunity to view new technologies of deathcare like water cremation through theological lenses to account for the reverence shown to the human body in the processes of disposition alongside the technology's ability to work *with*, and not *against*, the earth's relationship with the bodies of the dead.

Human Composting

In the early 1800s, the soil and bones from small urban churchyard burial grounds were used as fertilizer. Tons of human remains from churchyards were sent from London north to be used as rich fertilizer in hopes of clearing space in the burial ground for new burials. In Boston, one 1832 observer noted that "mouldering bodies have been battered to nourish vegetation"—a practice that continued for decades.[36] While this practice was largely frowned upon at the time, seen as disrespectful of the dead who likely did not know their decomposed remains would be removed from their graves and used as fertilizer, turning human remains into rich soil for fertilization is experiencing new popularity.

Human composting, tested in a 2018 study at Washington State University with donated human cadavers and first legalized for public use in Washington state, is a relatively simple process of "organic reduction" recognizable to anyone familiar with composting. The corpse is placed within an eight-by-four-foot steel cylinder with natural ingredients that speed the decomposition process: alfalfa, straw, and wood chips. The cylinder slowly rotates to enable oxygenation and mixing of the contents of the cylinder. The carbon, nitrogen, moisture, and microbes speed up the process of decomposition for the entire body—including bones—to a period of about one month.[37]

Human composting speeds up the natural process of decomposition rather than subverting it through flame cremation or delaying it through embalming and sealing the body in a casket and a vault. It also uses one-eighth the energy of cremation, and according to its inventor, Katrina Spade, each body composted rather than cremated saves over a metric ton of CO_2.[38] In an era when the earth has lost half of its topsoil in the last 150 years, creating nutrient-rich compost from our bodies represents a moral return of our mortal remains to a more-than-human web of life.[39] Spade's process, known as Recompose, yields one cubic yard of nutrient-rich soil. Families wishing to have this compost-like material to use on their own properties and gardens can take it away. But Recompose also offers families the opportunity to donate the compost remains to Bells Mountain, a seven-hundred-acre nonprofit land trust in southern Washington, to contribute to the revitalization of the forest and wetlands there.[40]

This process is reminiscent of the words of feminist environmental theorist Donna Haraway, who says, "We are compost, not posthuman. . . . Critters—human and not—become-with each other, compose and decompose each other, in every scale and register of time and stuff in sympoietic tangling, in ecological evolutionary developmental earthly worlding and unworlding."[41] Caitlin Campbell and Karla Rothstein make this process of sympoietic tangling palpably clear in relation to the corpse: "The corpse is a contradiction, simultaneously dead and energetic. Death triggers new biological and chemical processes; some of the estimated thirty-nine trillion bacterial cells that live on and in us shift into an active ecosystem of decomposition to begin the work of dismantling the body and redistributing its building blocks."[42]

Human composting enables this sympoietic tangling of (de)composition in a way that supports the processes of our becoming-with the larger web of life but without the use of land for natural burial. This is especially important in urban areas that have become heavily dependent upon flame cremation and those for whom a nearby green burial ground may be unavailable. While this deathcare practice is currently only available in three states in 2021—Washington, Oregon, and Colorado—religious communities have the opportunity to join with other community advocacy groups in support of legislation in making it more widely available in other parts of the country.

Home Funerals and Communal Care of the Dead

It was once the deceased person's family and wider community that took responsibility to care for the body after death. This communal praxis of deathcare is still quite typical among Muslims in the United States as well as many Jewish communities. But Christian communities—as well as our secular counterparts—have largely given over care for our dead to a professionalized chain of events in which we play a very small direct role.

But the practice of communal deathcare is not dead. In fact, it is experiencing quite a resurrection.[43] While Jewish and Muslim communities in the United States have never abdicated communal responsibility for deathcare or lost the knowledge necessary to undertake these sacred duties, Christian communities have little collective memory to rely on when it comes to caring for our own dead. We've abdicated these duties to a professional class of morticians and have forgotten much of what we once knew. But a new class of deathcare workers has emerged by various names that are not yet standardized and often in flux: death midwives, death doulas, and now, more commonly, home funeral guides and after-death care educators. Increasingly, the term *death doula* or *end-of-life doula* refers to those who assist the dying and their families before death, and "after-death care educator" refers to those who provide assistance and support after death has occurred. These guides educate families and communities on end-of-life and deathcare practices and, while not able to charge a fee for service in direct deathcare and funeral preparations, come alongside families to help them recover the knowledge and skills needed to care for a loved one's body in death, most often in the home.

As noted in chapters 1 and 2, from ancient Judaism through early Christianity and in the cultures of Native Americans and European settlers, women played a central role in caring for the dead throughout most of mortuary history leading up to the professionalization and industrialization of deathcare. At this time, women were displaced by men, who became central to the undertaking of a professional service rather than a familial or communal deathcare practice. However, a process of women-led reclamation of deathcare has begun. Lee Webster, a leader in the green burial and home funeral movements, points to the fact that women have been spearheading the social movements to promote home funerals since the 1990s, advocating for "more affordable, socially and environmentally responsible, family-centered after-death care."[44] She continues, "We are beginning to recognize that the very tasks that we have been outsourcing tether us to the reality of our changed world and the emotional pain that is the catalyst for grief . . . and give us a framework for tying all the threads of our lives back together."[45] Helping families tie these threads back together is the hope of home funerals and communal deathcare.

The home funeral movement, or communal care of the dead, is related to a larger death positivity movement that helps people reengage in conversations, decisions, processes, and practices related to the end of life.[46] Rather than positioning loved ones as helpless in the face of grief, home funerals engage them actively in the process of caring for their own dead. Sometimes, these activities involve a funeral director for some aspects of care (a few states *require* a funeral director for some aspect of the deathcare process).[47] In other instances, the family and their community undertake the entirety of the deathcare process on their own or with the help of a home funeral guide. More and more, funeral directors are also seeing the importance of providing services that foreground the family in the work of deathcare, and some now offer support to families in conducting home funerals or vigils.[48] A home funeral can eventuate in flame or water cremation, conventional burial, green burial, or human composting.

Home funerals allow families to set the pace of mourning and ritualizing the death of their loved one rather than working around the schedule or taken-for-granted chain of events at a funeral home. They allow everyone involved to feel useful in the work of deathcare—from children decorating a burial container with art, to those making food for mourners, to the loved ones involved in the sacred task of washing and preparing the body to be laid out at home. In this process of care, the family and community determine the tempo, typically slow and deliberate, allowing time for reflection and the flow of emotions and events that occur surrounding death. This experience-near process of deathcare normalizes death as a part of life and diminishes the fear that can develop for those long kept at a distance from the realities of death. Additionally, home funerals can help educate children about the life cycle and involve them in the process of communal grief and mourning in significant and meaningful ways.[49]

The dead body is many things to different people in different times and places: a site of personhood or lack thereof, a symbolic object, a ritual actor, an object to manipulate throughout the process of grief, a nurturing seed for the earth, a potent reminder of mortality, a sacred object, both host and guest of funeral rituals, a pure vessel, an object of decay and disorder, human but also not, an object communicating absence, an object connoting presence. The close engagement with the dead facilitated by home funerals and vigils and communal practices of deathcare creates the opportunity to make meaning with others not only of the life of the deceased but also in relation to their mortal remains—meaning constructed in communal acts of care for a beloved one knit in a web of care for and with their community in life and now in death.

There is ample room in this movement of communal deathcare for religious communities that see this as a vital ministry of care. Churches can develop the capacity to engage in advocacy alongside congregants experiencing a loss in order to help them make decisions around deathcare so that they are not pressured into making decisions they otherwise would not have made. Faith communities can engage in regular deathcare conversations with members to increase awareness of the availability of options in deathcare praxis to decrease the likelihood that some simply may not know what to do at the time of a loved one's death. And on the most active end of engagement, churches and other religious communities may consider developing community care groups with members trained in home funeral guide skills through the myriad workshops, conferences, and training opportunities now available. Threshold circles from faith communities can hold space for loved ones when death is imminent through gentle acts of care or the provision of music at the bedside of the dying and can even accompany loved ones who wish to care for the bodies of their dead in the hours or even days after a death has occurred.

Whatever form of corpse care a family or religious community engages in for their dead, religious communities, particularly the Christian communities that are the primary focus of this study, need to develop and/or sustain rituals that "honor the bodies of those who have departed."[50] The Christian corpse has reached its next step in the journey of faith. As Tom Long has observed, Christian faith "draws together all the necessity and custom of death into a funeral that bears witness to the gospel: a baptized saint, a child of God, one who has been traveling the path of faith is now 'traveling on.'"[51] As our sibling in faith moves along the last mile of the way, a community of companions in Christ can travel alongside to the place of farewell: "As we travel, we sing and pray, we tell once again the gospel story, we say farewell, and in faith, we return this our friend to God with thanksgiving."[52]

Deathcare has long been well within the purview of churches and communities of faith. It is only in the recent century of our long Christian history that we have largely abdicated this area of ministry to outside professionals. At this critical juncture in American deathcare, churches should be in the midst of the burgeoning options becoming available to families and communities who wish to reengage a Christian praxis of care for the dead.[53]

Other Notable Practices

Whenever we talk about our research with individuals and groups, we often hear statements like "Oh, yes. I want to become a tree when I die! Do you know about the tree burial pod?" Or "Have you heard of the mushroom suit? That seems so cool." And while these practices are often shared on social media as cutting-edge new deathcare practices, we have not dealt with them here because they are not widely in use and seem to us like boutique deathcare options with no more impactful ecological or meaning-making effects than the emerging practices we have explored above (not to mention their high cost).[54]

There is also a pluriform range of practices emerging on the edges of the death positivity movement and deathcare praxis, like the eating of cremation remains, the mixing of cremation ash with tattoo ink, and two embalmers in Ohio who will preserve the tattooed skin of dead loved ones and return it to the family as a keepsake. Shannon Lee Dowdy says of her anthropological research into these practices, "The more I worked on this project, the more I realized that, for a growing number of Americans, honoring the dead means deliberately breaking taboos. It's as if it is a necessary step in redefining the realm of the sacred. And what is becoming sacred are tiny fragments of the body, down to its chemical essence."[55] In some ways, many of these practices seem like a secularized, modern reminder of ancient practices of collecting relics from saintly religious figures, only in these instances, the figures are our own loved ones.

Notably, we have also omitted the discussion of whole-body donation to medical institutions for teaching or research. As a matter of practicality, we will note to the reader that while this is an admirable option for one to choose for one's corpse, there are circumstances in which one's body might not meet the acceptance criteria of an institution upon death. For example, the Mayo Clinic lists a few of these circumstances as the presence of an infectious or contagious disease, extreme emaciation or obesity, the necessity of an autopsy, or situations of mutilation or decomposition.[56] Thus, if whole-body donation to a medical facility is one's desired first choice for body disposition, one should *also* have an alternative plan in place should whole-body donation not become possible for any reason.

A Method for Future Theological Deathcare Deliberation

While our modern, conventional form of burial reigned as the standard practice for a hundred years and flame cremation is quickly surpassing it in popularity as a standard choice, the future of deathcare is likely not going to be a monolith. It seems clear at present that some mixture of natural burial, DIY home funerals, the traditional funeral home, cremation, standard conventional burial, water cremation, human composting, and other emerging options will exist side by side for some years to come. The near future of deathcare will be pluriform, an interweaving of practices and rituals and traditions—new practices emerge, the old becomes new again, and communities ritualize death with in-person and digital and hybrid forms of mourning. These practices will comingle in the years to come to form the twenty-first-century landscape of deathcare in the United States.

Each of these options, however, is not equal in its meaning, its ecological impact, its ability to facilitate a community's grief, or the ideologies that the practices either reify or refuse. They are not equally morally weighted nor equally theologically rich for a diversity of religious communities. Judgments must be made about our deathcare practices by individuals, families, and discerning communities. In our theological and ethical assessment, the practices that seem most theologically rich and communally meaningful in the time to come are those that honor the importance of our embodiment (even in death), practices of disposition that work with the earth and not against it, and rituals that cultivate a communal ethic of care in death as in life.

While we cannot anticipate the myriad of deathcare practices that are still to come, we offer to communities a brief method for thinking through the theological and ethical implications of practices that may emerge in the future. This method has five components, easily remembered with the acronym EARTH: ecological, anthropological, relational, technological, and health/harm/healing.[57] We offer these as questions communities might ask about future practices that emerge to facilitate the process of corpse care:

Ecological

- What are the desires of the earth in relation to the corpse, and how does this practice facilitate or subvert those desires?
- How is the dead body positioned in relation to the earth and the wider web of life in this practice?
- Does the practice place the body in connection to the earth or subvert the body/earth connection?

Anthropological

- How is the dead body positioned in relation to the living human community and its practices of grief and grieving?
- What institutions and social assemblages are in relationship with the dead body?
- Where does the "authority" over the dead rest in this practice?
- How does the practice facilitate or subvert the potential of a living community relating to the body of the dead?
- How can families and friends of the dead body be effectively integrated into the funeral service?

Relational

- How is the dead body put in relationship to time and space? For example, what is the relationship between the corpse and the wider web of life and among the dead, the living, and those yet to come?
- What kinship connections are considered in this practice across spiritual, spatial, and temporal dimensions?
- To whom is the corpse "related," and how does this practice honor and facilitate those relationships?

- What are the best practices when it comes to integrating deathcare into the Christian funeral liturgy, and what do our liturgical practices communicate about our relational imaginings (between the living and the dead, between our bodies and the earth, etc.)?

Technological

- What technologies are employed to address the dead body?
- How do these technologies facilitate or subvert connection within the ecological, anthropological, and relational dimensions of this method?
- Who is in charge of these technologies and how they are deployed, at what cost, and to whom?
- How are the technologies of deathcare assessed in relation to ecological, racial, cultural, and economic concerns of justice?

Health/Harm/Healing

- How is "health" conceived in relation to the dead body (e.g., healthy connections with the bodies of the dead, healthy grieving practices, presumed concerns of public health)? And who is making these determinations of health?
- What "harms" are imagined for humans and for other-than-human beings in the larger web of life in relation to the dead body and the practice under consideration?
- What practices of "healing" are being called for in order to address these presumed harms and their effects?
- How are the living and the dead and the larger web of life brought together, or not, by this practice?

In the pluriform landscape of deathcare to come, thoughtful, engaged, and caring communities of faith must reclaim their role in care for bodies across the life span, including in death. Corpse care has for too long been outside of our awareness as a concern for Christian care and theological deliberation. Now we must engage in the process of remembering the communal skills we have too willingly forgotten and develop the theological imagination to push beyond the status quo into meaningful ministry with our dead.

Conclusion

We are living and dying amid a tangle of old deathcare practices that no longer feel quite right to many families, a funeral industry trying to keep up in order to justify its presumed place at the center of deathcare in America, a burgeoning of death-tech inventiveness and deathcare (re)imagination that has not yet solidified in our collective consciousness, and a cadre of communal deathcare practitioners helping families reclaim their place in the deathcare scene. Yet churches are largely silent on our concern for the corpse. We must interrogate our silences as much as our speech.

Churches do not know how to think about the body theologically, much less the *dead* body. Feminist, womanist, queer, and disability theologians have long attempted to rectify this deficit when it comes to *living* bodies. We must now develop our theological abilities to confront our aversion to theologizing the *dead* body.

We're embarrassed by death, preferring to focus on the living. We've culturally moved from funerals with a dead body present, to bodiless memorial services to remember our dead, to celebrations of life in which the confrontation of death is held at bay by memories of happier times. For many churches, too much focus on death may distract from a feel-good, triumphant Christianity in which no limitation—not the limits of the ecosphere nor the limits of death—can curtail our conquering spirit. This certainly has its secular counterpart in the "transhumanist urge," which seeks to find ways to cure humanity of the need to die by expanding possibilities for life beyond our biological embodiedness through cryogenically freezing dead bodies for future reanimation or the melding of human consciousness with yet-to-come technologies.[1]

In our embarrassment over death, we theologically disregard the body for an escape to the heavenly clouds, or we technologically denigrate the body in hopes of being uploaded to the Cloud. But as Norman Wirzba argues, "The longing to escape to somewhere else mistakenly substitutes relocation for redemption. The point of faith, at least from a Christian point of view, is not simply to get somewhere else but to participate in and experience God's transforming presence in every place. Heaven, in other words, is not 'up beyond the blue.' It is wherever the love of God is at work."[2]

No matter our varied beliefs about an afterlife, theological or technological, the corpse remains as the materiality of our mortal existence and demands that we attend to it. Our care for the corpse, communally enacted and carefully situated within the web of life that entangles it, is an expression of the love of God at work.

Unlike many of our forebears in faith, however, we have difficulty remembering our own deaths, at least in an embodied fashion. Absent regular contact with corpses, attendance at funerals, or visits to our dead in burial grounds and cemeteries, we must cultivate our attention differently for a contemporary memento mori, to remember our deaths and the death of all we love.

Memento Mori in the Twenty-First Century

In January 2020, the Bulletin of the Atomic Scientists—keepers of the "Doomsday Clock" since 1947—moved the hand on the clock from its 2018 position of two minutes till midnight to just one hundred seconds till midnight, indicating our proximity to a catastrophic human-made threat to our very existence. In this case, the bulletin's science and security board are most concerned by the simultaneous existential threats of nuclear war and climate change, both now compounded by "cyber-enabled information warfare" that "undercuts society's ability to respond."[3]

This followed just over a year after the warning of the Intergovernmental Panel on Climate Change (IPCC) that the world has only until 2030 to take drastic action to reduce CO_2 levels by 45 percent to avert irreversible climate-driven disaster. With over six thousand scientific references, the 2018 IPCC report warned of catastrophic consequences if the global net CO_2 levels do not quickly fall by that drastic measure. This is a feat that would "require rapid, far-reaching and unprecedented changes in all aspects of society."[4]

On April 29, 2020, during the first wave of the Covid-19 pandemic, various news outlets reported that some one hundred corpses were discovered in two unrefrigerated rental trucks outside a funeral home in Brooklyn, New York.[5] Outrage soon followed. Brooklyn borough president Eric Adams tweeted, "We demand decent treatment of our deceased."[6] This story epitomizes the way in which the pandemic has focused our national and global attention on the care, or neglect, of corpses and the range of responses such (in)attention evokes. It will no doubt transform the ways we think about our responsibilities to, and treatment of, the deceased in the future. But this is not the first time larger cultural trends and crises have shaped corpse care. The questions "What is a corpse?" and "What is its proper treatment?" are not new questions, and responses to them have not been uniform.

The sick died without the presence of family or friends at the bedside in quarantined hospital ICUs. With hospital morgues full, refrigerated trailers were pulled into parking lots in order to contain the growing number of dead. New York City opened mass graves on Hart Island—a historic resting place for the city's unclaimed poor and victims of epidemics from Spanish flu to AIDS—now welcoming the unclaimed bodies dead of Covid-19.[7] Funeral practices during the pandemic were altered at a moment's notice to accommodate the care of the dead and the facilitation of grief.[8] The internet became a pervasive new means for mourning among family and friends who participated in funerals from a distance, often aided by the suddenly vital funerary accouterment of the livestreaming webcam or the Zoom funeral.[9]

The coronavirus pandemic that emerged on the world scene in 2019 and hit the United States with full force in early 2020 brought to the forefront of our minds and hearts the centrality of death as a human experience that could be brought near to any one of us at any time. Predictably, however, the pandemic disproportionately affected persons along familiar lines of racial inequality and economic disparity. In the United States alone, 112,700 people died of Covid-19 in the span of the first five months, with many cities bearing the weight of so many corpses that typical administrative means of "disposition" were no longer possible.[10] A few months into 2022, the death toll in the United States rose to 1 million, and the worldwide dead numbered well over 6 million, while Omicron, an even more highly transmissible variant of the virus, is still spreading across the planet.

Then in the midst of the pandemic, the world's attention was suddenly arrested by a viral video of the Black body of George Floyd being asphyxiated by police pressing his body into the pavement with a knee on his neck until he died pleading for mercy in front of onlooking crowds. From all over the world, we watched him die that May evening in Minneapolis. Over and over again, we witnessed life becoming death before our eyes. And we knew that his living body should not have become a dead body in the eight minutes and forty-six seconds that the police spent killing him before the eyes of the world.

I can't breathe officer
don't kill me
they're gonna kill me, man
come on man
I cannot breathe
I cannot breathe
they're gonna kill me
they're gonna kill me
I can't breathe
I can't breathe
please sir
please
please
please I can't breathe

These, Floyd's last words, and his body lying on the asphalt, pressed into the ground by the weight of the police officers on his back and neck, reactivated the dis-ease lodged in the racially rent soul of America. The ferment of movements for racial justice building for decades erupted in a vortex of activity, drawing in many more concerned and outraged and heartbroken citizens of every race than had ever before been active in the movement for Black lives.

Floyd's last words brought back to our collective awareness the 2014 New York police killing of Eric Garner, who pleaded "I can't breathe" until he suffocated from the officer's chokehold. Floyd's body-now-dead lying on the pavement of that Minneapolis street triggered the memory of the 2014 police shooting of Michael Brown in Ferguson, Missouri. Aside from Brown's killing by police—a reality the United States already knew intimately when it came to Black lives encountering law enforcement—it was his body-now-dead lying on the hot asphalt for four hours in front of his family and his friends, in front of his own mother pleading for the police to pick up her son's body, that heaped indignity on top of injustice.

Death confronts us—memento mori—on individual, societal, and planetary scales. Death challenges us to see our own social sins: racial and environmental, materialistic and militaristic. Death reminds us of what we've tried to forget: that we are caught up in an entangled web of living and dying. And amid death's confrontations, the corpse holds the ability to *do* something and not just *be* something. The corpse confronts us with the limitations of our human hubris. The corpse awakens us to our transcendent entanglement in our ecological home. The corpse galvanizes us to protest death-dealing injustice. The corpse engages communities in sacred practices of care. The corpse, in an ironic fashion, points us to life.

The Aliveness of the Corpse in a Web of Life on the Brink

We give our dead
To the orchards
And the groves.
We give our dead
To life.[11]

In our death, our body continues to experience what biologist and philosopher Andreas Weber terms the "aliveness" of the "shared and cocreated biosphere" of which we are a part. Aliveness, he continues, "is that which desires its own way of transformation before any conscious choice."[12] In an odd and ironic twist of composing and decomposing, of worlding and unworlding, the body can become animated by aliveness even in its death. In fact, death may promote a quality of "aliveness" unlike any we could experience in life: caring for the earth by receiving from the earth its final gift, doing for us what we cannot do for ourselves, returning the human to the humus, embedding our embodiedness in the cocreated biosphere of which we are a part. Death is integral to the process of our bodily *becoming*. Our incarnate bodies hold a desirous beingness-toward-death. And in that deathly becoming, even our dead bodies and the web of life that enfolds them hold a desirous beingness-toward-life again.

Our human disconnection from the web of life is at the root of why we do not see the value of connection to our dead through their return to the earth and our need for meaningful practices of corpse care. We are meant to (de)compose, to become-with the larger web of life, even in our death. Wendell Berry describes an experience of being very much alive in a way that intimates the process of decomposition of the body in the "dark proposal of the ground." He writes,

> And now a leaf, spiraling down in wild flight, lands on my shirt at about the third button below the collar. . . . Suddenly, I apprehend in it the dark proposal of the ground. Under the fallen leaf my breastbone burns with imminent decay. Other leaves fall. My body begins its long shudder into the humus. I feel my substance escape me, carried into the mold by beetles and worms. Days, winds, seasons pass over me as I sink under the leaves. For a time only sight is left me, a passive awareness of the sky overhead, birds crossing, the mazed interreaching of the treetops, the leaves falling—and then, that, too, sinks away. It is acceptable to me, and I am at peace. When I move to go, it is as though I rise up out of the world.[13]

Even in decay, our bodies long "to participate in and experience God's transforming presence in every place," as Wirzba describes the "point of faith."[14] It echoes in the words of Joseph Story at the founding of Mount Auburn Cemetery, declaring that solace, even pleasure, can be gained from the knowledge "that when the hour of separation comes, these earthly remains will still retain the tender regard of those whom we leave behind;—that the spot, where they shall lie, will be remembered with a fond and soothing reverence."[15] And it resounds in the consecration hymn of those gathered to open that cemetery:

Here to thy bosom, mother Earth,
Take back, in peace, what thou hast given;
And all that is of heavenly birth,
O God in peace, recall to heaven![16]

Our participation in and experience of God's transforming presence in every place—even in death—is even more pertinent for a planet in climate crisis.

Our deathcare practices have always shifted in times of crises: epidemics of disease that left too many dead for the living to care for by traditional means often resulted in mass graves. Population booms leaving cities overcrowded with burial grounds too full to contain more bodies shifted burial outside of city centers to rural landscapes. Civil War soldiers dying for the first time en masse away from home, piling up on battlefields, resulted in preserving practices of embalming to return bodies to families and professionals to do for the dead what families were typically too far away to do.

Now our own crises have become too obvious to escape: anthropogenic climate change and ecological destruction, extreme weather wreaking havoc across the world, a worldwide pandemic that, despite a herculean scientific effort, has seemed unrelenting for a matter of years. The crisis that most profoundly shifted deathcare praxis in America was once centered on the separation of living communities from their dead, who were dying away from home during the Civil War. We now live and die amid a crisis of our human separation from the ecological web of life in a context of death in which we are all caught up, human and other-than-human alike.

While our deathcare practices will not save us, what we do at the limit-experience of death is instructive to us, communicating our relational values and theological ethics that become cemented over time. Cutting ourselves off in death from the aliveness of the web of life has mirrored the trajectory of our most destructive human tendencies. We must now develop practices of deathcare that reshape our relationship with our own bodies and the body of the earth. Our deathcare praxis to come must narrate the theology, the ethics, and the communal values that we most need at this critical moment in history. Communities of faith should be at the very center of these efforts because what we must communicate in the face of death is of theological significance on the largest scale and is good news to a planetary web of life on the brink.

In our deathcare, we must embody the truth that our most fundamental material relationship is with the soil. From humus to human is our theological origin story of embodiment. When we make decisions about our bodies in death, we must recognize that the earth's desire has for too long been subjugated to human appetites. And in death, the earth's desire is for our bodies to be given back to it: from humus to human to humus again. In our deathcare praxis, our communal role in caring for the dead provides an opportunity to do for others what they cannot do for themselves, engaging us in acts of care for a beloved one in death as in life. And in our death, our bodies continue to be entangled in a web of life that is still in the process of becoming: life becoming death and transforming into life yet again.

We must give our dead to life.

Notes

Introduction

1 Erik R. Seeman, *Death in the New World: Cross-Cultural Encounters, 1492–1800* (Philadelphia: University of Pennsylvania Press, 2010), 52.
2 A term that Seeman uses that is inclusive of "deathbed scenes, corpse preparation, burial practices, funerals, mourning, and commemoration." Seeman, 1.
3 Seeman, 52.
4 Seeman, 94–95.
5 Drew Gilpin Faust, *This Republic of Suffering: Death and the Civil War* (New York: Vintage Books, 2008), xvii.
6 Faust, 102. Historian Thomas W. Laqueur, *The Work of the Dead: A Cultural History of Mortal Remains* (Princeton, NJ: Princeton University Press, 2015), argues, "The impulse to recover the special if not the ordinary dead goes back to the beginning of the writing of history" (33).
7 Elizabeth Outka, "'Wood for the Coffins Ran Out': Modernism and the Shadowed Afterlife of the Influenza Pandemic," *Modernism/Modernity* 21, no. 4 (2015): 937.
8 Outka, 938.
9 Karla F. C. Holloway, *Passed On: African American Mourning Stories* (Durham, NC: Duke University Press, 2003), 58.
10 Holloway, 60.
11 It is also helpful to remember that even the final "disposition" of dead bodies bespeaks the divisions of a society, as bodies that have been objects of prejudice and injustice in life throughout the history of the United States are made so again in death. Cemeteries weren't desegregated until a 1968 Supreme Court

ruling in *Jones v. Mayer* (Holloway, 203). For a history of African American cemeteries, see Roberta Hughes Wright and Wilbur B. Hughes III, *Lay Down Body: Living History in African American Cemeteries* (Detroit: Visible Ink, 1996).

12 Achille Mbembe, *Necropolitics* (Durham, NC: Duke University Press, 2019), 36.

13 Lauren DeLand, "Live Fast, Die Young, Leave a Useful Corpse: The Terrible Utility of David Wojnarowicz," *Performance Research* 19, no. 1 (March 2014): 34.

14 DeLand, 36.

15 Judith Butler, *Notes toward a Performative Theory of Assembly* (Cambridge, MA: Harvard University Press, 2015), 197.

16 This will take on a particular character as a *theological* process of becoming, but death researchers in other fields have similar ways of relating to death. For example, "cultural sociology systematically challenges reifying perspectives and suggests that death should be conceived of as a becoming," argue Tora Holmberg, Annika Jonsson, and Fredrik Palm, "Introduction: Why Death Matters," in *Death Matters: Cultural Sociology of Mortal Life*, ed. Tora Holmberg, Annika Jonsson, and Fredrik Palm (Cham, Switzerland: Palgrave Macmillan, 2019), 9.

17 Andreas Weber, *Enlivenment: Toward a Poetics for the Anthropocene* (Cambridge, MA: MIT Press, 2019), 23.

18 Cicero, *Tusc.* I.43, trans. J. E. King, LCL 141 (Cambridge, MA: Harvard University Press, 1927). Interestingly, and this will be pertinent to future chapters, Diogenes' views about what to do with his dead body emerged not from a devaluation of the body, as many might have understood through the ages, but instead from what Thomas Laqueur describes as Diogenes's views on living a virtuous life, which included the notion that a virtuous person "ought to comport himself as closely as possible to nature." Laqueur, *Work of the Dead*, 37.

19 "Statistics," National Funeral Directors Association, accessed June 30, 2020, https://www.nfda.org/news/statistics.

20 To put this in a larger perspective, the largest multinational funeral conglomerate, Service Corporation International (SCI), reported to the US Securities and Exchange Commission $3,190,200,000 in revenue in 2018. US Securities and Exchange Commission, accessed February 1, 2021, http://investors.sci-corp.com/phoenix.zhtml?c=108068&p=irol-reportsAnnual.

21 Though these are important concerns we will return to, how we use money in relation to death, as an exertion of agential power in relation to the death of our body to make happen what we believe ought to happen, is of central theological importance. As Henri Nouwen persuasively argues, "Money and power go together. There is also a real relationship between power and a sense of self-worth. Do we ever use money to control people or events? In other words, do we use our money to make things happen the way we want them to happen?" See Henri J. M. Nouwen, *A Spirituality of Fundraising* (Nashville: Upper Room Books, 2010), 30.

22 Davies uses the expression "words against death" to encapsulate a theory of death rites as an adaptation to the fact of death. Douglas Davies, *Death, Ritual and Belief: The Rhetoric of Funerary Rites*, 3rd ed. (London: Bloomsbury, 2017), 4.

23 Osmer names four helpful practical theological questions that will become important throughout the course of this book: "What is going on? Why is this

going on? What ought to be going on? How might we respond?" Richard R. Osmer, *Practical Theology: An Introduction* (Grand Rapids, MI: Eerdmans, 2008), 4.

24 Luke Timothy Johnson (*The Revelatory Body: Theology as Inductive Art* [Grand Rapids, MI: Eerdmans, 2015], 1) makes the connection between theology and the body, saying, "The human body is the preeminent arena for God's revelation in the world, the medium through which God's Holy Spirit is most clearly expressed . . . the task of theology is the discernment of God's self-disclosure in the world through the medium of the body." As Gordon D. Kaufman argues, "In saying that we are to begin with 'God's revelation,' it is assumed that we know what we are talking about when we say 'God' and 'revelation,' and that there is nothing problematical about these terms." Here, in a pragmatist practical theological vein, we begin with the dead body as a site of theological inquiry to, as Kaufman later expresses, "discern and formulate explicit criteria and procedures for theological construction." See Gordon D. Kaufman, *An Essay on Theological Method*, 3rd ed. (Atlanta: Scholars Press, 1995), 3, 44.

25 So argues Gordon D. Kaufman in *The Problem of God* (Cambridge, MA: Harvard University Press, 1972), 46–49. We might also recall here that it was the disputed question of death that stood at the nexus between the first humans in the garden of Eden, the crafty serpent, and the Creator God (Gen 3:1–4).

26 As Sanders has elsewhere said, "Caskets and vaults and other funerary accouterments are our final act of withholding our bodies from their potential to nurture the earth and, instead, consuming the ultimate panoply of 'things' we don't need. Perhaps they satiate our capitalistic need to 'do something' by 'buying something' when the thing that actually needs doing—caring for the bodies of our dead by returning something sacred to where it belongs—is removed from the hands of loved ones, and corpses are withheld from the ecosystem to which they belong." Cody J. Sanders, "Mor(t)al Remains: Pastoral Theology and Corpse Care," *Journal of Pastoral Theology* 29, no. 2 (2019): 9.

27 Sanders has elsewhere described the "good death" as "the way we'd want to die if we had our druthers. Our notions of the Good Death are informed by our cultural landscape and, for many, by our religious imaginaries. Typically, the Good Death is an approximation of the kind of death most people of some racial and economic privilege in the society enjoy." See Cody J. Sanders, "How the Covid-19 Pandemic May Permanently Change Our 'Good Death' Narrative," *Religion Dispatches*, April 20, 2020, https://religiondispatches.org/how-the-covid-19-pandemic-may-permanently-change-our-good-death-narrative/.

28 Importantly, while our inquiry is a theological one, these questions are not limited to religious communities or those professing a particular faith. Ekerwald's research demonstrated that secular interviewees who believed that they would be nonexistent after death still held concerns about how they would be represented and perceived after death, including how their dead bodies would be treated. He states, "Treating a person in a dignified way and also treating that person's dead body in a dignified way are two actions that are linked. I interpret this to mean that a secular person who believes that death means the individual ending still wants to treat the body of the dead person with respect and veneration. If you respect people, you respect their dead bodies. This respect for the dead body is

not linked to religion. Death invites veneration among us all." Hedvig Ekerwald, "Me and My Dead Body: Death, Secularism, and Simultaneity," in Holmberg, Jonsson, and Palm, *Death Matters*, 160.

1: The Corpse from Antiquity to Antebellum Garden Cemeteries

1 Tob 1:18; Josephus, *J.W.* 5.514; *Jub* 23:23.

2 Lucian, *Luct.* 21, trans A. M. Harmon, LCL 162 (Cambridge, MA: Harvard University Press, 1925).

3 Diogenes Laertius, *Lives* 6.2.79, trans. R. D. Hicks, LCL 185 (Cambridge, MA: Harvard University Press, 1925). Thomas Laqueur uses Diogenes as a foil throughout his magisterial volume *Work of the Dead* (3–5 passim) to challenge the notion of the importance of the corpse and its proper care.

4 Matt 8:21–22; Luke 9:59–60.

5 Grave robbers might also be included among those who exhibited disregard for the corpse in antiquity. While such acts of impiety could include profanation of the corpse itself (which, at a minimum, included the exposure of a nude, decaying body), they were generally aimed at the illegal acquisition of the tomb accouterments intended to accompany the deceased on their journey. See especially Éric Rebillard, "Violation of Tombs and Impiety: Funerary Practices and Religious Beliefs," in *The Care of the Dead in Late Antiquity*, trans. Elizabeth Trapnell Rawlings and Jeanine Routier-Pucci, Cornell Studies in Classical Philology 59 (Ithaca, NY: Cornell University Press, 2009), 57–88. One early Christian caveat is found at the third/fourth-century Catacomb of Saint Agnes in Rome: "May whoever violates this tomb die a terrible death, lie unburied, never rise again, and share the fate of Judas"; *Inscriptiones Christianae Urbis Romae* (*ICVR*) 8.21396; cited by Rebillard, *Care of the Dead*, 75.

6 Herodotus, *Hist.* 2.85, trans. A. D. Godley, LCL 118 (Cambridge, MA: Harvard University Press, 1921).

7 Egyptians were not the only ones accused of necrophilia in antiquity. While such accounts are not frequent, they are not altogether missing from ancient accounts; cf. J. L. Lightfoot, *Parthenius of Nicaea* (Oxford: Clarendon Press, 1999), 535.

8 Herodotus, *Hist.* 2.89 (Godley); cf. Xenophon of Ephesus, *The Story of Anthia and Habrocomes* 5.9–11.

9 Carl H. Kraeling, "Was Jesus Accused of Necromancy?," *JBL* 59, no. 2 (1940): 147.

10 1 Sam 28. For other examples, see Daniel Ogden's *Magic, Witchcraft, and Ghosts in the Greek and Roman Worlds: A Sourcebook* (Oxford: Oxford University Press, 2009).

11 J. M. C. Toynbee, *Death and Burial in the Roman World* (Ithaca, NY: Cornell University Press, 1971), 43–44. Toynbee gives references to primary literature for each of the actions described here. Admittedly, this is a blunt and coarse frame of reference, since it does not take into account differences in geographical location, social and economic status, and gender. See also Valerie Hope, who has commented insightfully on the difficulties in deciphering the available evidence. Valerie Hope, *Roman Death: The Dying and the Dead in Ancient Rome* (New York: Continuum, 2009), 65–66.

12 Presumably, this would include also Ananias and Sapphira, who were landowners in the early church (Acts 5).
13 Luke 7:11–17.
14 Luke 9:9.
15 Luke 9:59–60.
16 Luke 23:50–53.
17 Luke 8:49–56.
18 Luke 13:1–5.
19 Acts 1:3.
20 Acts 1:18–19.
21 Acts 5:1–11.
22 Acts 8:2.
23 Acts 9:36–43.
24 Acts 12:2.
25 Acts 12:23.
26 Acts 20:9.
27 Acts 22:4; 26:9, 13. There are also expressions of readiness for death (Simeon, Luke 1:29; Paul, Acts 21:13), a near suicide (the Philippian jailor, Acts 16:23), and a plot to assassinate Paul (Acts 23:12–21).
28 See Craig Keener, *Acts: An Exegetical Commentary*, vol. 2 (Grand Rapids, MI: Baker Academic, 2013), 2:1471–82.
29 Acts 9:36–42.
30 Acts 9:37.
31 Acts 9:40.
32 *m. Sabb.* 23:5, trans. Herbert Danby, *The Mishnah: Translated from the Hebrew with Introduction and Brief Explanatory Notes* (Oxford: Oxford University Press, 1933).
33 See A.-J. Levine, "Tabitha / Dorcas, Spinning Off Cultural Criticism," in *Delightful Acts: New Essays on Canonical and Non-canonical Acts*, ed. Harold W. Attridge, Dennis R. MacDonald, and Clare K. Rothschild, WUNT 391 (Tübingen: Mohr Siebeck, 2017), 41–65.
34 Homer, *Il.* 18.343–53, trans. A. T. Murray, rev. William F. Wyatt, LCL 171 (Cambridge, MA: Harvard University Press, 1925; emphasis added); cf. 24.582–83. For other references to corpse washing, see Virgil, *Aen.* 6.219; Martial, *Epigr.* 9.57.8; Juvenal, *Sat.* 3.171–72; cf. Keener, *Acts*, 2:1716n119.
35 Luke 23:56; 24:1.
36 *T. Ab.* 20:11.
37 *m. Sabb.* 23:5; Homer, *Il.* 18.343–53.
38 Luke 23:53.
39 Acts 5:6.
40 *m. Kil.* 9:4; *Ma'as. Š.* 5:12; *Ned.* 2:7; *Nid.* 9:17. See Shemuel Safrai, "Home and Family," in *The Jewish People in the First Century*, ed. S. Safrai and M. Stern (Amsterdam: Van Gorcum, 1976), 2:776–77.
41 See also Cicero, *Fam.* 4.12.3; Statius, *Silv.* 2.1.157–62; and *Apoll. K. Tyre* 26.
42 Luke 7:11–17.
43 Luke 7:12.
44 The substantive participle, βαστάζοντες, simply means to lift or carry and is used in a variety of contexts in the New Testament and even in Luke/Acts (Luke 10:4; 11:27; 14:27; 22:10; Acts 3:2; 9:15; 15:10; 21:35).

45 Persius, *Sat.* 3.105–6; Philostratus, *Vit. soph.* 2.1.565–66.
46 Martial, *Epigr.* 8.75.9; Toynbee, *Death and Burial*, 46.
47 Tob 4:3–4; 6:15; 4 Macc 16:11; Demosthenes, *I Aristog.* 54; Quintilian, *Decl.* 302.4.
48 Luke 9:59–60.
49 Diogenes Laertius, *Lives* 6.2.78.
50 Luke 23:53. According to Jodi Magness, burial caves were accessible only to the wealthier citizens in Jerusalem. The "poorer members of Jerusalem's population apparently disposed of their dead in a manner that has left fewer traces in the archaeological record: for example, in individual trench graves or cist graves dug into the ground." Jodi Magness, "Ossuaries and the Burials of Jesus and James," *JBL* 124, no. 1 (2005): 123.
51 For the funerary obligations, financial and otherwise, of a Greco-Roman voluntary association and its possible connections to early "associations" of Jesus followers, see John Kloppenborg, *Christ's Associations: Connecting and Belonging in the Ancient City* (New Haven, CT: Yale University Press, 2019), 265–77.
52 Acts 5:1–11.
53 See Magness, "Ossuaries and the Burials," 123; and Toynbee, *Death and Burial*, 46.
54 Lucian, *On Funerals*, trans. A. M. Harmon, LCL 162 (Cambridge, MA: Harvard University Press, 1925), 11; cf. Herodotus, *Histories* 2.85.
55 Keener, *Acts*, 2:1477.
56 See Cicero, *Fam.* 9.20.3; Cicero, *Tusc.* 3.62; Plutarch, *Cons. Ux.* 4; Tacitus, *Agr.* 29.1; and Seneca, *Polyb.* 17.4–6. Cited by Hope, *Roman Death*, 209n6, 210n10. Lucian (*Luct.* 12) criticized the excessive "wailing of women" at funerals. Elites might also have paid musicians, mimes, and/or mourners. For more on idealized and ritualized grieving, see Hope, "Mourning the Dead," in *Roman Death*, 121–49.
57 Luke 23:48; cf. also 23:27.
58 Acts 8:2.
59 Acts 9:39; also Jairus's daughter, if she were truly dead and not sleeping (Luke 8:52).
60 Seneca, *Ep. Lucil.* 99; *m. Sanh.* 6:6.
61 Caroline Walker Bynum, *The Resurrection of the Body in Western Christianity, 200–1336* (New York: Columbia University Press, 2017), 53, 55. This practice, and ones similar to it, led to charges of cannibalism against Christians (Eusebius, *Ecc. Hist.* 5.1).
62 Contra the older work by James Spencer Northcote, William R-Brownlow, and Giovanni Battista De Rossi, *Roma Sotterranea: Or, Some Account of the Roman Catacombs* (London: Longman, Green, Reader and Dyer, 1869) and with Rebillard, *Care of the Dead.*
63 Bynum, *Resurrection*, 58.
64 Phillipe Aries, *Western Attitudes toward Death: From the Middle Ages to the Present*, trans. Patricia M. Ranum (Baltimore: Johns Hopkins University Press, 1974), 14–18.
65 Bynum, *Resurrection*, 318.
66 Bynum, 321. Cf. also N. T. Wright, *The Resurrection of the Son of God* (Minneapolis: Fortress, 2003).
67 Bynum, 321, 326. At the same time, there was also an increase in mutilation as a punishment for capital crimes.

68 *Deathways* is a term that includes "deathbed scenes, corpse preparation, burial practices, funerals, mourning, and commemoration." Seeman, *Death in the New World*, 1.
69 Native Americans in other parts of the country had different burial customs. The Plains Indigenous peoples of Oklahoma, for example, often used caves for burial sites and sometimes exposed bodies on mesas to allow animals to consume them.
70 Seeman, *Death in the New World*, 13, 170.
71 Seeman, 14.
72 Seeman, 144–45.
73 Seeman, 193–94.
74 Seeman, 106–7.
75 Seeman, 128.
76 Christina Sharpe, *In the Wake: On Blackness and Being* (Durham, NC: Duke University Press, 2016), 21.
77 Seeman, *Death in the New World*, 7.
78 Seeman, 95.
79 Seeman, 95.
80 Seeman, 175.
81 Seeman, 85.
82 Seeman, 91.
83 Gary Laderman, *The Sacred Remains: American Attitudes toward Death, 1799–1883* (New Haven, CT: Yale University Press, 1996), 6.
84 Sharpe, *In the Wake*, 38.
85 Laderman, *Sacred Remains*, 11.
86 David E. Stannard, *The Puritan Way of Death: A Study in Religion, Culture, and Social Change* (New York: Oxford University Press, 1977), 100–101, 108–9.
87 Stannard, 103, 107.
88 Stannard, 109–10.
89 Stannard, 122.
90 Laderman, *Sacred Remains*, 30.
91 Stannard, *Puritan Way of Death*, 111–12.
92 Laderman, *Sacred Remains*, 29.
93 Laurel K. Gabel, "Death, Burial, and Memorialization in Colonial New England: The Diary of Samuel Sewall," *Markers* 25 (2008): 25.
94 Gabel notes the little-known custom that midwives and nurses were often the ones given the honor of preparing the corpse of a stillborn baby and carrying the coffin to the grave. Gabel, 19.
95 Stannard, *Puritan Way of Death*, 112–13.
96 Stannard, 113. In addition to the published materials cited here, we are also grateful to June Hobbs and Laurel Gabel for their education on the gravestones and burial grounds of New England as we explored these sites alongside them.
97 It is notable that, according to Gabel, fewer than half of Boston's burials from this period were marked with permanent gravestones. Gabel, "Death, Burial, and Memorialization," 13. For more on the artistry and iconography of New England grave markers, see Allan I. Ludwig, *Graven Images: New England Stonecarving and Its Symbols 1650–1815* (Middletown, CT: Wesleyan University

Press, 1966); Dickran Tashjian and Ann Tashjian, *Memorials for Children of Change: The Art of Early New England Stonecarving* (Middletown, CT: Wesleyan University Press, 1974); and Thomas E. Gilson and William Gilson, *Carved in Stone: The Artistry of Early New England Gravestones* (Middletown, CT: Wesleyan University Press, 2012).

98 Stannard, *Puritan Way of Death*, 113, 115.

99 Stannard, 129.

100 Laderman, *Sacred Remains*, 42–43.

101 Stannard, *Puritan Way of Death*, 135.

102 Stannard, 150.

103 For a much more in-depth history of ecclesiastical authority over the corpse in Europe, see Laqueur, *Work of the Dead.*

104 Laderman, *Sacred Remains*, 50.

105 For example, hundreds of patents were taken out between 1850 and 1880 for new forms of caskets that replaced the traditional coffin. These were far more elaborate and far more expensive than the wooden coffin had been up to this point in history. Stannard, *Puritan Way of Death*, 188.

106 Laderman, *Sacred Remains*, 46. *Casket* is a word originally meaning "jewel box." Stannard, *Puritan Way of Death*, 188.

107 Blanche M. G. Linden, *Silent City on a Hill: Picturesque Landscapes of Memory and Boston's Mount Auburn Cemetery* (Amherst: University of Massachusetts Press, 2007), 147.

108 For a helpful contextualization of Mount Auburn and the rural cemetery movement within the larger landscape of American environmentalism in the nineteenth century, see Aaron Sachs, *Arcadian America: The Death and Life of an Environmental Tradition* (New Haven, CT: Yale University Press, 2013).

109 For more on this, see Sachs, 33.

110 One contemporary example is the number of people who do not attend church but prefer to have some traditional religious elements performed in their funeral services.

111 Stannard, *Puritan Way of Death*, 162–63.

112 Linden, *Silent City on a Hill*, 9.

113 Linden, 118–19.

114 Linden, 130.

115 Linden, 128.

116 Linden, 10.

117 Linden, 144.

118 Quoted in Linden, 26.

119 Linden, 95–116.

120 Linden, 187, 190.

121 Laderman, *Sacred Remains*, 78.

122 Laderman, 82. For a helpful assessment of the corpse in medical discourse to the present day, see Jeffrey P. Bishop, *The Anticipatory Corpse: Medicine, Power, and the Care of the Dying* (Notre Dame, IN: University of Notre Dame Press, 2011).

123 Laderman, *Sacred Remains*, 81.

124 For a thorough assessment of industrialization as well as the contemporary economy and our relationship to care for the dead, see Candi K. Cann, *Virtual*

Afterlives: Grieving the Dead in the Twenty-First Century (Lexington: University Press of Kentucky, 2014).

125 Joseph Story, "An Address Delivered on the Dedication of the Cemetery at Mount Auburn, September 24, 1831," Mount Auburn Cemetery, September 24, 2011, https://mountauburn.org/joseph-storys-consecration-address/.

126 Nancy West, "Pictures of Death," *Atlantic*, July 19, 2017, https://www.theatlantic.com/technology/archive/2017/07/pictures-of-death/534060/.

127 Linden, *Silent City on a Hill*, 180.

128 Laderman, *Sacred Remains*, 65.

129 Laderman, 169–70.

130 Linden, *Silent City on a Hill*, 81.

131 Aaron Sachs argues, "At the precise moment when Western society seemed to focus itself most powerfully on the death-denying conquest and harnessing of nature, some members of that society were using landscapes of death to preach a humble acknowledgement of natural limitations." Sachs, *Arcadian America*, 22–23.

132 "Hymn Sung at Consecration," Mount Auburn Cemetery, August 1, 2014, https://mountauburn.org/hymn-sung-at-consecration/.

133 Jacob Bigelow, *A History of the Cemetery at Mount Auburn* (Boston: James Munroe, 1860), 176, quoted in Sachs, *Arcadian America*, 31. Another quote from Bigelow worth rendering in full was from a speech to the Boston Society for the Promotion of Useful Knowledge in 1831, the year of Mount Auburn's founding:

> The plant which springs from the earth, after attaining its growth and perpetuating its species, falls to the ground, undergoes decomposition, and contributes its remains to the nourishment of plants around it. The myriads of animals which range the woods or inhabit the air, at length die upon the surface of the earth, and if not devoured by other animals, prepare for vegetation the place which receives the remains. Were it not for this law of nature, the soil would be soon exhausted, the earth's surface would become a barren waste, and the whole race of organized beings, for want of sustenance, would become extinct. (Bigelow, *History*, 176–77, quoted in Sachs, *Arcadian America*, 31)

134 Jessica Bussmann, "Notable 'Green' Residents of Mount Auburn," Mount Auburn Cemetery, August 26, 2012, https://mountauburn.org/eternally-green-green-notables/.

135 Linden, *Silent City on a Hill*, 136.

136 Linden, 175.

137 Linden, 46.

138 Laderman, *Sacred Remains*, 47.

139 Laderman, 66–67.

140 Laderman, 67.

2: The Corpse from the Civil War to the Industrialization of Deathcare

1 Seeman, *Death in the New World*, 194–96.

2 Seeman, 19–21.

3 Seeman, 21.
4 For a poignant accounting of slave ship journeys, see Sharpe, *In the Wake*.
5 Seeman, *Death in the New World*, 188–89.
6 Seeman, 213, 220–21.
7 Seeman, 204–5. For a more thorough exploration of the history of many African American cemeteries in the United States, see Roberta Hughes Wright and Wilbur B. Hughes III, *Lay Down Body: Living History in African American Cemeteries* (Detroit: Visible Ink, 1996).
8 Seeman, *Death in the New World*, 227.
9 Claudia Rankine, "The Condition of Black Life Is One of Mourning," in *The Fire This Time: A New Generation Speaks about Race*, ed. Jesmyn Ward (New York: Scribner, 2016), 145–46.
10 For more on the Cambridge Mount Auburn Cemetery's relationship with race, see Friends of Mount Auburn, "African American Heritage Trail," Mount Auburn Cemetery, February 1, 2013, https://mountauburn.org/african-american-trail/.
11 Kami Fletcher, "Founding Baltimore's Mount Auburn Cemetery and Its Importance to Understanding African American Burial Rights," in *Till Death Do Us Part: American Ethnic Cemeteries as Borders Uncrossed*, ed. Allan Amanik and Kami Fletcher (Jackson: University Press of Mississippi, 2020), 130.
12 Fletcher, 130.
13 Fletcher, 131.
14 Jeffrey E. Smith, "Till Death Keeps Us Apart: Segregated Cemeteries and Social Values in St. Louis, Missouri," in Amanik and Fletcher, *Till Death Do Us Part*, 163.
15 Fletcher, "Founding Baltimore's Mount Auburn Cemetery," 146.
16 Laura Harjo, *Spiral to the Stars: Mvskoke Tools of Futurity* (Tucson: University of Arizona Press, 2019), 148.
17 Laderman, *Sacred Remains*, 33, 38.
18 Faust, *This Republic of Suffering*, 9.
19 Faust, 10.
20 Faust, 11.
21 Laderman, *Sacred Remains*, 27–28.
22 Faust, *This Republic of Suffering*, xvi. However, twice as many soldiers died of disease than the wounds of war (4).
23 Faust, 62.
24 Laderman, *Sacred Remains*, 98.
25 Faust, *This Republic of Suffering*, 71–72, 102.
26 Faust, 16.
27 Faust, 29.
28 Faust, 24.
29 Laderman, *Sacred Remains*, 143.
30 Faust, *This Republic of Suffering*, 90.
31 Faust, 102. It was the Civil War that instituted the practice of dedicating a system of national cemeteries to honor the military dead (103).
32 Faust, 85.
33 Faust, 241.
34 Mary Bradbury observed, "We can clearly see why the lack of a body to manipulate and to mourn over causes such consternation. We have been robbed of the

very object with which we articulate our sacred and profane representations of death." Mary Bradbury, *Representations of Death: A Social Psychological Perspective* (New York: Routledge, 1999), 138.

35 Laderman, *Sacred Remains*, 113–14.
36 Laderman, 165–66.
37 Faust, *This Republic of Suffering*, 94.
38 Faust, 95 (emphasis in original).
39 Laderman, *Sacred Remains*, 101.
40 Laderman, 154.
41 Laderman, 157.
42 Additionally, Enlightenment perspectives on the body and the relationship between death and natural processes contributed to a decrease in theological perspectives on the centrality of the corpse in death; see Laderman, 137.
43 Laderman, 137.
44 Laderman, 141.
45 Laderman, 169.
46 Laderman, 47.
47 Laderman, 8.
48 Laderman, 174.
49 Gary Laderman, *Rest in Peace: A Cultural History of Death and the Funeral Home in Twentieth-Century America* (New York: Oxford University Press, 2003), 9, 100.
50 Laderman, 102.
51 Holloway, *Passed On*, 16–17.
52 Holloway, 23.
53 Holloway, 25.
54 Holloway, 181.
55 Laderman, *Rest in Peace*, 32.
56 Laderman, 70.
57 Laderman, 24.
58 Laderman, *Sacred Remains*, 174.
59 Laderman, 30.
60 Holloway, *Passed On*, 23.
61 Laderman, *Rest in Peace*, 61–70.
62 "Certified Celebrant Training," National Funeral Directors Association, accessed June 19, 2021, https://nfda.org/education/certification-training-programs/about-certified-celebrant-training.
63 Stephen Prothero, *Purified by Fire: A History of Cremation in America* (Berkeley: University of California Press, 2001), 4.
64 Prothero, 9–10.
65 Prothero, 57, 77.
66 Prothero, 86, 97. It is ironic to note that cremation got a boost in the United States from immigrants for whom it was already a tradition of deathcare (e.g., Sikhs in the early twentieth century). See Prothero, 127.
67 For more on the ecological impact of cremation, see "Disposition Statistics," Green Burial Council, accessed June 19, 2021, https://www.greenburialcouncil.org/media_packet.html.
68 Prothero, *Purified by Fire*, 83–84.

69 Prothero, 142.
70 Laderman, *Rest in Peace*, 143. There is also a connection, mentioned elsewhere, between cremation and AIDS activism. In 1996, an activist from the group ACT UP threw an urn containing the remains of a man who had died of AIDS over the fence of the White House to protest the AIDS policies of President Bill Clinton. Prothero, *Purified by Fire*, 198.
71 Prothero, *Purified by Fire*, 200.
72 Cann, *Virtual Afterlives*, 18.
73 For a helpful overview of the differences between lawn park and memorial park cemeteries, see "1900–Present: Lawn-Park Cemeteries and Memorial Parks," Pennsylvania Historical and Museum Commission, August 26, 2015, http://www.phmc.state.pa.us/portal/communities/cemetery-preservation/development/1900-present.html.
74 Sachs, *Arcadian America*, 35.
75 See "Investor Overview," Service Corporation International, accessed June 19, 2021, https://investors.sci-corp.com.
76 "Investor Fact Sheet," Service Corporation International, accessed June 19, 2021, https://filecache.investorroom.com/mr5ir_scicorp/194/Investor-Fact-Sheet%202020%20Q4%20FINAL.pdf.
77 "Where Do Americans Die?," Palliative Care, Stanford School of Medicine, accessed June 9, 2021, https://palliative.stanford.edu/home-hospice-home-care-of-the-dying-patient/where-do-americans-die/.
78 Sarah H. Cross and Haider J. Warraich, "Changes in the Places of Death in the United States," *New England Journal of Medicine*, December 12, 2019, https://www.nejm.org/doi/full/10.1056/NEJMc1911892.
79 "Statistics." In 2019, the number of funeral homes in the United States was 19,136, approximately 89.2 percent of which were privately owned, with another 10.8 percent owned by publicly traded corporations like Service Corporation International, the largest funeral service conglomerate.
80 Mark Everly, "When Someone Dies, What Happens to the Body?," Conversation, September 15, 2020, https://theconversation.com/when-someone-dies-what-happens-to-the-body-143070.
81 For a detailed account from a funeral professional, see Everly.
82 "Statistics."
83 "Statistics."
84 Sara Marsden-Ille, "What Is the Average Cost of a Cremation?," US Funerals Online, November 26, 2020, https://www.us-funerals.com/what-is-the-average-cost-of-a-cremation/#.YMDK-i-cbdc.
85 "Grave Liner and Vault Options," Pine Hill Cemetery Association, accessed June 9, 2021, http://pinehillcemeterydavenport.com/media//DIR_4401/7b2aa0364051e060ffff804effffe904.pdf.
86 "The FTC Funeral Rule," Federal Trade Commission Consumer Information, July 2012, https://www.consumer.ftc.gov/articles/0300-ftc-funeral-rule.
87 "The Cremation Process from Start to Finish," Lincoln Heritage Funeral Advantage, accessed June 9, 2021, https://www.lhlic.com/consumer-resources/how-does-cremation-work/#long.
88 Cann, *Virtual Afterlives*, 4.

3: The Corpse in the Web of Life

1 See Elizabeth Kolbert, *The Sixth Extinction: An Unnatural History* (New York: Henry Holt, 2014).

2 "Media Release: Nature's Dangerous Decline 'Unprecedented'; Species Extinction Rates 'Accelerating,'" Intergovernmental Science-Policy Platform on Biodiversity and Ecosystem Services, accessed June 23, 2021, https://www.ipbes.net/news/Media-Release-Global-Assessment.

3 We are not naive to the difficulties surrounding this term. While *Anthropocene* points to the role of *humanity's* contributions to climate change and ecological destruction, the term also hides the fact that it is not *all* of humanity that has made this anthropogenic impact upon the earth. It is disproportionally wealthy, industrialized nations that have made this degrading impact on the environment, leading some to point to *capitalism* or *colonialism* rather than "humanity" as the primary culprit. This has given rise to other terms for our current era, such as *Capitalocene*, *Plantatiocene*, or *Eurocene*. As will hopefully become clear, though we use the term *Anthropocene*—as an important concept within geology and the environmental humanities—we strive to nuance just what contexts and factors of human activity contribute most to the picture of human-ecological relationship we are developing.

4 See Harvey Cox, *The Market as God* (Cambridge, MA: Harvard University Press, 2016).

5 Suzanne Kelly expands this argument in *Greening Death: Reclaiming Burial Practices and Restoring Our Tie to the Earth* (New York: Rowman & Littlefield, 2015).

6 Walter Brueggemann, *The Land: Place as Gift, Promise, and Challenge in Biblical Faith*, 2nd ed. (Minneapolis: Fortress, 2002), xi.

7 For example, see Brueggemann; and Ellen F. Davis, *Scripture, Culture, and Agriculture: An Agrarian Reading of the Bible* (Cambridge: Cambridge University Press, 2008).

8 Deut 30:16–19; cf. 8:17–20.

9 Ps 24:1.

10 Gal 3:6–8; cf. Rom 4:2.

11 This is the conclusion of W. D. Davies in his classic treatment, *The Gospel and the Land: Early Christianity and Jewish Territorial Doctrine* (Berkeley: University of California Press, 1974).

12 Davis, *Scripture, Culture, and Agriculture*, 8.

13 Davis, 31. Davis draws on, and is in dialogue with, contemporary agrarian writers, especially Wendell Berry, who wrote the preface to Davis's book.

14 Rom 8:19–23; cf. also Col 1:15–20. David Horrell et al. refer to, and complicate, these two texts as the "ecotheological 'mantra' texts"; cf. David G. Horrell, Cherryl Hunt, and Christopher Southgate, *Greening Paul: Rereading the Apostle in a Time of Ecological Crisis* (Waco, TX: Baylor University Press, 2010), esp. 63–116.

15 Cf. 1 Cor 15:35–49. This is a somewhat convoluted argument by Paul; at the least, though, it presumes the dead body returns to the earth as "a man of dust" (1 Cor 15:47).

16 For a helpful examination of the liturgical dimensions of the human relation to the earth in funerary ritual, see Benjamin M. Stewart's "Committed to the Earth: Ecotheological Dimensions of Christian Burial Practices," *Liturgy* 27, no. 2 (2012): 62–72; and Benjamin M. Stewart's "The Place of the Earth in Lutheran Funeral Rites: Mapping the Current Terrain," *Dialogue: A Journal of Theology* 52, no. 2 (2014): 118–26.

17 Eccl 3:19–20.

18 Eccl 9:12.

19 Anna Krzywoszynska and Greta Marchesi, "Toward a Relational Materiality of Soils," *Environmental Humanities* 12, no. 1 (2020): 192.

20 "Soil Erosion and Degradation: Overview," World Wildlife Fund, accessed March 31, 2019, https://www.worldwildlife.org/threats/soil-erosion-and-degradation.

21 Robert Pogue Harrison, *The Dominion of the Dead* (Chicago: University of Chicago Press, 2003), x.

22 Harrison, xi.

23 Jamie Lorimer, "Rot," *Environmental Humanities* 8, no. 2 (2016): 237.

24 Lorimer, 235.

25 Carl Jung, *Man and His Symbols* (London: Aldus Books, 1964), 95.

26 One might also mention disability studies as another impetus in the turn toward the body; cf., e.g., Nancy L. Eiesland, *The Disabled God: Toward a Liberatory Theology of Disability* (Nashville: Abingdon, 1994); and Deborah Beth Creamer, *Disability and Christian Theology: Embodied Limits and Constructive Possibilities* (Oxford: Oxford University Press, 2009). Reilly Cosgrove, Sarah Barton, and Devan Stahl, "Disability Theology: A Working Bibliography," *The Faithful OT*, accessed June 16, 2022, https://thefaithfulot.com/resources/.

27 Jane Barter Moulaison, "'Our Bodies, Our Selves?' The Body as Source in Feminist Theology," *SJT* 60 (2007): 342.

28 Moulaison, 342. Karen J. Warren, "The Power and Promise of Ecological Feminism," *Environmental Ethics* 12 (1990): 125–46. Moulaison offers a typology of two feminist approaches to "embodied discourse." The "organic body" recognizes that "all our knowledge, including our moral knowledge is body-mediated knowledge. All knowledge is rooted in our sensuality" (Beverly Wildung Harrison, "The Power of Anger in the Work of Love: Christian Ethics for Women and Other Strangers," *USQR* 36 [1981]: 48). For the "subversive body," the body's significance "is not in its ability to 'make the connections' with others and with nature; but rather to offer bodily performances which resist the social dictates of sexual and gendered behavior" (Moulaison, "'Our Bodies, Our Selves?,'" 345). Both moves—organic and subversive—run the risk of describing the body as an "abstraction."

29 These are the chapter titles of Johnson's *Revelatory Body*. Johnson also included a critique of John Paul II's *Theology of the Body: Human Love in the Divine Plan* (New York: Pauline Books and Media, 1997) under the title "The Way Not Taken: A Disembodied Theology of the Body" (21–36).

30 Johnson, *Revelatory Body*, 7.

31 Paul J. Griffiths, *Christian Flesh* (Stanford, CA: Stanford University Press, 2018), 5.

32 Griffiths, 9.
33 Alexis Shotwell, *Against Purity: Living Ethically in Compromised Times* (Minneapolis: University of Minnesota Press, 2016), 7.
34 G. W. F. Hegel, *The Philosophy of History*, trans. J. H. Clarke (New York: Dover, 1956). See also Ronald Kuykendall, "Hegel and Africa: An Evaluation of the Treatment of Africa in the Philosophy of History," *Journal of Black Studies* 23 no. 4 (1993): 572.
35 Joshua Lederberg and Alexa T. McCray, "'Ome Sweet 'Omics—a Genealogical Treasury of Words," *Scientist* 15, no. 7 (2001): 8. For more on the human microbiome, see Jane Peterson et al., "The NIH Human Microbiome Project," *Genome Research* 19, no. 12 (2009): 2317–23, https://www.ncbi.nlm.nih.gov/pmc/articles/PMC2792171/#B13.
36 Jane Bennett, *Vibrant Matter: A Political Ecology of Things* (Durham, NC: Duke University Press, 2010), 112–13.
37 Sally McFague, *The Body of God: An Ecological Theology* (Minneapolis: Fortress, 1993).
38 Bruno Latour, *Facing Gaia: Eight Lectures on the New Climatic Regime*, trans. Catherine Porter (Medford, MA: Polity, 2017), 13.
39 Shotwell, *Against Purity*, 11.
40 Shotwell, 11–12.
41 While other concerns may rise to the top of our advocacy agenda, Christina Staudt and Karla Rothstein make clear the—albeit sometimes unconscious—centrality of our approaches to death in ways that impact myriad other concerns: "Consciously recognized or not, the inevitability of death is foundational to cultural manifestations and production, and influences personal predilection and acquired thought. It drives basic survival measures, spurs legacy inclination, mobilizes us to placate threatening forces, and intensifies empathy." Karla Rothstein and Christina Staudt, introduction to *The Future of the Corpse: Changing Ecologies of Death and Disposition*, ed. Karla Rothstein and Christina Staudt (Santa Barbara, CA: Praeger, 2021), xv.
42 John Boopalan, "'Will the Dust Praise You?': Theologizing Death," *Political Theology Network*, June 21, 2021, https://politicaltheology.com/will-the-dust-praise-you-theologizing-death/?fbclid=IwAR3FzwAEfRR6nqwKSx5G_RUdNTh9cAlp7g4FsoE-BbktikW90EMO2AQ4tHw.
43 "First Nations in Central B.C. Honour Children Discovered at Kamloops Residential School," CBC News, June 20, 2021, https://www.cbc.ca/news/canada/british-columbia/first-nations-in-central-b-c-honour-children-discovered-at-kamloops-residential-school-1.6072828.
44 Ian Austen and Dan Bilefsky, "In Canada, Another 'Horrific' Discovery of Indigenous Children's Remains," *New York Times*, June 24, 2021.
45 Eric Hanson, Daniel P. Games, and Alexa Manuel, "The Residential School System," *Indigenous Studies UBC*, September 2020, https://indigenousfoundations.arts.ubc.ca/the_residential_school_system/#what-were-residential-schools.
46 See "Missing and Murdered Indigenous Women," Native Hope, accessed November 15, 2021, https://www.nativehope.org/en-us/understanding-the-issue-of-missing-and-murdered-indigenous-women.
47 Harjo, *Spiral to the Stars*, 34.

48 Shotwell, *Against Purity*, 37.
49 Shotwell, 60.
50 Chanequa Walker-Barnes, "Response to Rev. Michael McBride Plenary, 'Conversions in the Age of Trump' Society for Pastoral Theology, June 14, 2018," *Journal of Pastoral Theology* 29, no. 1 (2019): 13.
51 Walker-Barnes, 13.
52 Holloway, *Passed On*, 10.
53 Maureen Corrigan, "'Let the People See': It Took Courage to Keep Emmett Till's Memory Alive," NPR, October 30, 2018, https://www.npr.org/2018/10/30/660980178/-let-the-people-see-shows-how-emmett-till-s-murder-was-nearly-forgotten.
54 "About CRDS," Collective for Radical Death Studies, accessed November 13, 2021, https://radicaldeathstudies.com/about-crds/. Readers may also be interested in the Queer Death Studies Network, founded in 2016, which exists to "investigate and challenge conventional normativities, assumptions, expectations, and regimes of truths that are brought to life and made evident by death, dying, and mourning . . . researching and narrating death, dying and mourning in the context of queer bonds and communities." "About," Queer Death Studies Network, accessed November 13, 2021, https://queerdeathstudies.net.
55 John Erik Troyer, "Technologies of the HIV/AIDS Corpse," *Medical Anthropology* 29, no. 2 (2010): 135.
56 Troyer, 135.
57 Troyer, 137.
58 DeLand, "Live Fast, Die Young," 33.
59 DeLand, 36.
60 Troyer, "Technologies of the HIV/AIDS Corpse," 143.
61 Troyer adroitly describes the control that embalming gave to the funeral industry:

> The fundamental historical importance of mechanical embalming was that it stopped human decomposition by altering human biology and consistently produced a dead body that appeared unaltered by time. This fundamental shift in the nascent American funeral industry standardized an experience of the postmortem body that persists today. In simple terms, the mechanical modification of the dead body affected how an observer visually experienced the corpse and also came to alter Americans' popular understanding of how "natural" or "normal" death appeared. . . . Since the tools used to alter the corpse were largely invisible and the embalming process took place behind closed doors, the end result was a new kind of postmortem body that looked alive yet bore no visible marks of mechanical intervention. The sheer invisibility of the embalming tools meant that these mechanical apparatus could permanently attach itself to a viewer's understanding of a dead body without directly altering the observer's conscious, visual understanding of death. By the late nineteenth century, the corpse was no longer totally controlled by biological death; rather, human control of the corpse and the "death" that it presented were mediated by human actors. (Troyer, 138)

62 Ellen Stroud, "Law and the Dead Body: Is a Corpse a Person or a Thing?," *Annual Review of Law and Social Science* 14 (2018): 117.
63 Stroud, 117, 122.
64 See "History," GMHC, accessed November 20, 2021, https://www.gmhc.org/history/.
65 Justin Cook, "A Cemetery Angel and the American HIV/AIDS Crisis," Collective for Radical Death Studies, August 25, 2019, https://radicaldeathstudies.com/2019/08/25/a-cemetery-angel-and-the-american-hiv-aids-crisis/.
66 For more on death and materiality, see Holmberg, Jonsson, and Palm, "Introduction," 14.

4: The Corpse to Come

1 Donna Haraway defines this word thus: "*Sympoiesis* is a simple word; it means 'making-with.' Nothing makes itself; nothing is really autopoietic or self-organizing. . . . *Sympoiesis* is a word proper to complex, dynamic, responsive, situated, historical systems. It is a word for worlding-with, in company." See Donna J. Haraway, *Staying with the Trouble: Making Kin in the Chthulucene* (Durham, NC: Duke University Press, 2016), 58.
2 For a thorough history of natural, green, or woodland burial—especially as it pertains to its recent history in Britain—see Douglas Davies and Hannah Rumble, *Natural Burial: Traditional-Secular Spiritualities and Funeral Innovation* (New York: Continuum, 2012).
3 Billy Campbell, "Rest in Perpetual Wilderness," *Katúah Journal* 20 (1988): 14.
4 "Ramsey Creek Preserve History," Memorial Ecosystems, accessed December 6, 2021, https://www.memorialecosystems.com/ramsey_creek_preserve_history.html.
5 "Green Burial Council Cemetery Certification Standards," Green Burial Council, December 18, 2019, https://www.greenburialcouncil.org/our_standards.html. For conservation burial, see also Conservation Burial Alliance, accessed December 4, 2021, https://www.conservationburialalliance.org.
6 David Charles Sloane, "Nature versus Culture: Shifting Values in American Cemeteries," in *The Future of the Corpse: Changing Ecologies of Death and Disposition*, ed. Karla Rothstein and Christina Staudt (Santa Barbara, CA: Praeger, 2021), 129. Thanks to Lee Webster, who has personally kept track of the growing number of green burial grounds and provided us with her current count.
7 Harrison, *Dominion of the Dead*, 24.
8 Harrison, 25.
9 For more on this history, see Holloway, *Passed On*.
10 Diane Jones, "The City of the Dead: The Place of Cultural Identity and Environmental Sustainability in the African-American Cemetery," *Landscape Journal* 30 (2011): 234–35.
11 Jones, 234–35.
12 Norman Wirzba, *This Sacred Life: Humanity's Place in a Wounded World* (New York: Cambridge University Press, 2021), 14.
13 Achille Mbembe, *Critique of Black Reason*, trans. Laurent Dubois (Durham, NC: Duke University Press, 2017), 40.

14 Barbara A. Holmes, *Crisis Contemplation: Healing the Wounded Village* (Albuquerque, NM: CAC, 2021), 26. Womanist ethicist Melanie Harris also points to the parallels between the violation of enslaved women's bodies and the violation of the "body of the earth," both abused as a function of a logic of domination. Ecowomanism makes explicit the parallel between colonization practices exacted upon African bodies through the transatlantic slave trade and the colonization of the earth. Christian theologies play a central role in this logic of colonization. Melanie L. Harris, *Ecowomanism: African American Women and Earth-Honoring Faiths* (Maryknoll, NY: Orbis Books, 2017), 18. See also the connections made between ecojustice and Black liberation theology in James H. Cone, "Whose Earth Is It Anyway?," in *Earth Habitat: Eco-justice and the Church's Response*, ed. Dieter Hessel and Larry Rasmussen (Minneapolis: Fortress, 2001), 23–32.

15 Adam Searle, "Absence," *Environmental Humanities* 12, no. 1 (2020): 168.

16 Searle, 171.

17 Shannon Lee Dowdy, *American Afterlife: Reinventing Death in the 21st Century* (Princeton, NJ: Princeton University Press, 2021), 26. See also Merlin Sheldrake, *Entangled Life: How Fungi Make Our Worlds, Change Our Minds, and Shape Our Futures* (New York: Random House, 2020).

18 "Home," Honey Creek Woodlands, accessed December 4, 2021, https://www.honeycreekwoodlands.com.

19 "Buying a Plot/Pricing," Honey Creek Woodlands, accessed December 6, 2021, https://www.honeycreekwoodlands.com/buying-a-plot-1.

20 "Home," Heritage Acres Memorial Sanctuary, accessed December 4, 2021, https://www.heritageacresmemorial.org.

21 "Pricing List," Heritage Acres Memorial Sanctuary, accessed December. 6, 2021, https://www.heritageacresmemorial.org/pricing-2/.

22 Amy Knueven Brownlee, "Heritage Acres Memorial Sanctuary Is Our Area's Only Dedicated Natural Burial Preserve," *Cincinnati Magazine*, December 4, 2020, https://www.cincinnatimagazine.com/article/heritage-acres-memorial-sanctuary-is-our-areas-only-dedicated-natural-burial-preserve/.

23 Grace Church Natural Burial, accessed December 4, 2021, https://gracechurchsc.org/naturalburial/.

24 "Why Natural Burial," Grace Church Natural Burial, accessed December 4, 2021, https://gracechurchsc.org/naturalburial/why/.

25 "Frequently Asked Questions," Grace Church Natural Burial, accessed December 6, 2021, https://gracechurchsc.org/naturalburial/faq/.

26 A reference to John 4:35b. Individuals and faith communities desiring information to help in the cultivation of deathcare work—including green burial and home funeral care, addressed later in this chapter—should consult the following resources: J. Mark Barna and Elizabeth J. Barna, *A Christian Ending: A Handbook for Burial in the Ancient Christian Tradition*, 2nd ed. (Manton, CA: Divine Ascent Press, 2011); Lee Webster and Donna Belk, *Planning Guide and Workbook for Home Funeral Families* (Everett, WA: National Home Funeral Alliance, 2015); Lee Webster, ed., *Changing Landscapes: Exploring the Growth of Ethical, Compassionate, and Environmentally Sustainable Green Funeral Service* (Self-published, CreateSpace, 2016); Holly Stevens and Donna Belk, *Undertaken with Love:*

A Home Funeral Guide for Families and Community Care Groups (Everett, WA: National Home Funeral Alliance, 2016); Elizabeth Fournier, *The Green Burial Guidebook: Everything You Need to Plan an Affordable, Environmentally Friendly Burial* (Novato, CA: New World Library, 2018); and Mallory McDuff, *Our Last Best Act: Planning for the End of Our Lives to Protect the People and Places We Love* (Minneapolis: Broadleaf Books, 2021).

27 "Industry Statistical Information," Cremation Association of North America, accessed December 9, 2021, https://www.cremationassociation.org/page/IndustryStatistics.

28 See E. E. Keijzer and H. J. G. Kok, *Environmental Impact of Different Funeral Technologies* (Utrecht: TNO, 2011), 5, 18, as cited in Caitlin Campbell and Karla Rothstein, "New Mortuary Technologies and Memorial Designs," in *The Future of the Corpse: Changing Ecologies of Death and Disposition*, ed. Karla Rothstein and Christina Staudt (Santa Barbara, CA: Praeger, 2021), 227.

29 Martin Heidegger, "The Question Concerning Technology," in *The Question Concerning Technology and Other Essays*, trans. William Lovitt (New York: Harper & Row, 1977), 11, as cited in Mark I. Wallace, *When God Was a Bird: Christianity, Animism, and the Re-enchantment of the World* (New York: Fordham University Press, 2019), 55–56.

30 Wallace, *When God Was a Bird*, 56.

31 Wallace, 56.

32 Campbell and Rothstein, "New Mortuary Technologies," 228.

33 Delia Gallagher, Daniel Burke, and James Masters, "Vatican Issues Guidelines on Cremation, Says No to Scattering Ashes," CNN World, October 25, 2016, https://www.cnn.com/2016/10/25/europe/cremation-vatican-scattering/index.html.

34 Karen Mahoney, "Bishops Oppose 'Flameless Cremation' Bill," *Catholic Herald*, May 17, 2021, https://catholicherald.org/local/bishops-oppose-flameless-cremation-bill/.

35 Mahoney.

36 Linden, *Silent City on a Hill*, 25.

37 Campbell and Rothstein, "New Mortuary Technologies," 232.

38 Hallie Golden, "'Give Back to the Earth': Washington Could Legalize Composting of Human Remains," *Guardian*, March 12, 2019, https://www.theguardian.com/us-news/2019/mar/11/human-composting-after-death-washington?CMP=share_btn_link.

39 "Soil Erosion and Degradation." For Spade's work, see Recompose, https://recompose.life.

40 "Environmental Impact," Recompose, accessed December 10, 2021, https://recompose.life/our-model/#the-forest.

41 Haraway, *Staying with the Trouble*, 97.

42 Campbell and Rothstein, "New Mortuary Technologies," 233. See also Ed Young, *I Contain Multitudes: The Microbes within Us and a Grander View of Life* (New York: Ecco, 2016).

43 Cody Sanders is grateful to Pashta MaryMoon, Rochelle Martin, Anne Jungerman, and Lee Webster for early and formative education in and exposure to home deathcare movements and practices.

44 Lee Webster, "Rethinking the Role of the Funeral Director," in *The Future of the Corpse: Changing Ecologies of Death and Disposition*, ed. Karla Rothstein and Christina Staudt (Santa Barbara, CA: Praeger, 2021), 166. Notably, this resurgence of women in deathcare is also occurring in the funeral directing profession, with women representing around 60 percent of mortuary science students in the United States.

45 Webster, 155.

46 One prominent spokesperson within this larger movement is Caitlin Doughty, whose website, Order of the Good Death (https://www.orderofthegooddeath.com), and books have helped many approach various topics related to death and deathcare in an approachable way. See Caitlin Doughty, *From Here to Eternity: Traveling the World to Find the Good Death* (New York: Norton, 2017); and Caitlin Doughty, *Smoke Gets in Your Eyes: And Other Lessons from the Crematory* (New York: Norton, 2014).

47 See the National Home Funeral Alliance for further resources on communal deathcare and a directory of resources and home funeral guides (https://www.homefuneralalliance.org) as well as the National End-of-Life Duala Alliance (https://www.nedalliance.org/after_death_care.html).

48 We are deeply indebted to Wendy Eidson of Phoenix Funeral Services, Inc., in Conyers, Georgia, for her in-depth conversation about our research and her practices related to supporting families choosing home funerals and green burials. See Phoenix Funeral Services, Inc., https://www.phoenixfuneralservicesinc.com. Additionally, the Keefe Funeral Home of Cambridge and Arlington, Massachusetts, has developed the capacity to support families wishing to hold a home vigil and engage in care for their own dead prior to burial or cremation. See "Home Vigil Support," Keefe Funeral Home, accessed December 10, 2021, https://www.keefefuneralhome.com/home-vigil-support. Cody Sanders is grateful to Tim Keefe for inviting his students from Andover Newton Theological School into the funeral home to discuss his work in this regard.

49 Cody Sanders is grateful to Lee Webster for her insights represented in this paragraph shared in a lecture with his students at Andover Newton Theological School, "Home Funerals and Green Burial" (lecture, Andover Newton Theological School, Newton, MA, April 17, 2018).

50 Thomas G. Long, *Accompany Them with Singing: The Christian Funeral* (Louisville: Westminster John Knox, 2009), 7.

51 Long, 16–17. Tom Long and Thomas Lynch, among others, have provided thoughtful reflections on funeral liturgy and deathcare for Christian congregations; see, e.g., Thomas G. Long and Thomas Lynch, *The Good Funeral: Death, Grief, and the Community of Care* (Louisville: Westminster John Knox, 2013). See also Sanders, "Mor(t)al Remains," 116–31; and Stewart, "Place of the Earth," 118–26.

52 Long, *Accompany Them with Singing*, 16–17.

53 Many resources now exist to help individuals and communities build skills in home deathcare. For example, see Joshua Slocum and Lisa Carlson, *Final Rights: Reclaiming the American Way of Death* (Hinesburg, VT: Upper Access Books, 2011); Lisa Carlson, *Caring for the Dead: Your Final Act of Love* (Hinesburg, VT: Upper Access Books, 1998).

54 There are, however, other practices, like the use of cremated remains to build artificial coral reefs to submerge in the ocean where reefs are quickly dying, that seem interesting and of some ecological promise, yet we have not addressed them here. For more, see Mark Harris, *Grave Matters: A Journey through the Modern Funeral Industry to a Natural Way of Burial* (New York: Scribner, 2007).

55 Dowdy, *American Afterlife*, 35.

56 "Body Donation at Mayo Clinic," Mayo Clinic, accessed December 10, 2021, https://www.mayoclinic.org/body-donation/making-donation.

57 This method is more fully developed for other practical theological projects in Cody J. Sanders, "Decentering the Human in Practical Theologies of Care: An EARTH Method," *International Journal of Practical Theology*, in press.

Conclusion

1 For a trenchant theological critique of transhumanism, see Wirzba, *This Sacred Life*, 34–60.

2 Wirzba, 44.

3 "Closer Than Ever: It's 100 Seconds to Midnight," *Bulletin of the Atomic Scientists*, January 23, 2020, https://thebulletin.org/doomsday-clock/current-time/.

4 "Summary for Policymakers of IPCC Special Report on Global Warming of 1.5°C Approved by Governments," IPCC, accessed January 21, 2020, https://www.ipcc.ch/2018/10/08/summary-for-policymakers-of-ipcc-special-report-on-global-warming-of-1-5c-approved-by-governments/.

5 Morgan Winsor and Emily Shapiro, "US Coronavirus Death Toll Surpasses 60,000 and 100 Bodies Found in Trucks Outside NYC Funeral Home," ABC News, April 30, 2020, https://abcnews.go.com/Health/coronavirus-updates-us-federal-inmate-dies-covid-19/story?id=70399771.

6 Eric Adams (@BPEricAdams), "I'm heading out to Flatlands," Twitter, April 29, 2020, 4:59 p.m., https://twitter.com/BKBoroHall/status/1255602699841798157?ref_src=twsrc%5Etfw%7Ctwcamp%5Etweetembed%7Ctwterm%5E1255602699841798157%7Ctwgr%5E%7Ctwcon%5Es1_&ref_url=https%3A%2F%2Fwww.washingtonpost.com%2Fnation%2F2020%2F04%2F30%2Fuhaul-bodies-coronavirus%2F.

7 Elyse Samuels and Adriana Usero, "'New York City's Family Tomb': The Sad History of Hart Island," *Washington Post*, April 27, 2020, https://www.washingtonpost.com/history/2020/04/27/hart-island-mass-grave-coronavirus-burials/.

8 Jodi Kantor, "'We're Going to See What Else the Word Funeral Can Mean," *New York Times*, April 5, 2020, https://www.nytimes.com/2020/04/05/us/coronavirus-dilemmas-mourning.html; Sanders, "Covid-19 Pandemic"; Christina Schoenwetter, "When We Can't Gather, How Do We Mourn?," *Sojourners*, June 9, 2020, https://sojo.net/articles/when-we-cant-gather-how-do-we-mourn.

9 Though the internet had already become a mourning space in varied ways prior to the pandemic. See Cann, *Virtual Afterlives*.

10 "Daily Updates of Totals by Week and State: Provisional Death Counts for Coronavirus Disease 2019 (Covid-19)," Centers for Disease Control and Prevention, July 2, 2020, https://www.cdc.gov/nchs/nvss/vsrr/covid19/index.htm.

11 From Earthseed's *The Book of the Living*, in Octavia E. Butler, *Parable of the Talents* (New York: Grand Central, 1998), 5.
12 Weber, *Enlivenment*, 14, 28.
13 Wendell Berry, "A Native Hill," in *The Art of the Commonplace: The Agrarian Essays of Wendell Berry*, ed. Norman Wirzba (Berkeley, CA: Counterpoint Press, 2002), 31.
14 Wirzba, *This Sacred Life*, 44.
15 Story, "Address Delivered."
16 "Hymn Sung at Consecration."

Bibliography

Aries, Phillipe. *Western Attitudes toward Death: From the Middle Ages to the Present.* Translated by Patricia M. Ranum. Baltimore: Johns Hopkins University Press, 1974.

Austen, Ian, and Dan Bilefsky. "In Canada, Another 'Horrific' Discovery of Indigenous Children's Remains." *New York Times*, June 24, 2021.

Barna, J. Mark, and Elizabeth J. Barna. *A Christian Ending: A Handbook for Burial in the Ancient Christian Tradition.* 2nd ed. Manton, CA: Divine Ascent Press, 2011.

Bennett, Jane. *Vibrant Matter: A Political Ecology of Things.* Durham, NC: Duke University Press, 2010.

Berry, Wendell. "A Native Hill." Pages 3–31 in *The Art of the Commonplace: The Agrarian Essays of Wendell Berry.* Berkeley, CA: Counterpoint Press, 2002.

Bigelow, Jacob. *A History of the Cemetery at Mount Auburn.* Boston: James Munroe, 1860.

Bishop, Jeffrey P. *The Anticipatory Corpse: Medicine, Power, and the Care of the Dying.* Notre Dame, IN: University of Notre Dame Press, 2011.

Boopalan, John. "'Will the Dust Praise You?': Theologizing Death." *Political Theology Network*, June 21, 2021. https://politicaltheology.com/will-the-dust-praise-you-theologizing-death/?fbclid=IwAR3FzwAEfRR6nqwKSx5G_RUdNTh9cAlp7g4FsoE-BbktikW90EMO2AQ4tHw.

Bradbury, Mary. *Representations of Death: A Social Psychological Perspective.* New York: Routledge, 1999.

Brownlee, Amy Knueven. "Heritage Acres Memorial Sanctuary Is Our Area's Only Dedicated Natural Burial Preserve." *Cincinnati Magazine*, December 4,

2020. https://www.cincinnatimagazine.com/article/heritage-acres-memorial-sanctuary-is-our-areas-only-dedicated-natural-burial-preserve/.

Brueggemann, Walter. *The Land: Place as Gift, Promise, and Challenge in Biblical Faith*. 2nd ed. Minneapolis: Fortress, 2002.

Bulletin of the Atomic Scientists. "Closer Than Ever: It's 100 Seconds to Midnight." January 23, 2020. https://thebulletin.org/doomsday-clock/current-time/.

Bussmann, Jessica. "Notable 'Green' Residents of Mount Auburn." Mount Auburn Cemetery, August 26, 2012. https://mountauburn.org/eternally-green-green-notables/.

Butler, Judith. *Notes toward a Performative Theory of Assembly*. Cambridge, MA: Harvard University Press, 2015.

Butler, Octavia E. *Parable of the Talents*. New York: Grand Central, 1998.

Bynum, Caroline Walker. *The Resurrection of the Body in Western Christianity, 200–1336*. New York: Columbia University Press, 2017.

Campbell, Billy. "Rest in Perpetual Wilderness." *Katúah Journal* 20 (1988): 14.

Campbell, Caitlin, and Karla Rothstein. "New Mortuary Technologies and Memorial Designs." Pages 226–244 in *The Future of the Corpse: Changing Ecologies of Death and Disposition*. Edited by Karla Rothstein and Christina Staudt. Santa Barbara, CA: Praeger, 2021.

Cann, Candi K. *Virtual Afterlives: Grieving the Dead in the Twenty-First Century*. Lexington: University Press of Kentucky, 2014.

Carlson, Lisa. *Caring for the Dead: Your Final Act of Love*. Hinesburg, VT: Upper Access Books, 1998.

CBC News. "First Nations in Central B.C. Honour Children Discovered at Kamloops Residential School." June 20, 2021. https://www.cbc.ca/news/canada/british-columbia/first-nations-in-central-b-c-honour-children-discovered-at-kamloops-residential-school-1.6072828.

Centers for Disease Control and Prevention. "Daily Updates of Totals by Week and State: Provisional Death Counts for Coronavirus Disease 2019 (Covid-19)." July 2, 2020. https://www.cdc.gov/nchs/nvss/vsrr/covid19/index.htm.

Cicero. *Tusculan Disputations*. Translated by J. E. King. LCL 141. Cambridge, MA: Harvard University Press, 1927.

Collective for Radical Death Studies. "About CRDS." Accessed November 13, 2021. https://radicaldeathstudies.com/about-crds/.

Cone, James H. "Whose Earth Is It Anyway?" Pages 23–32 in *Earth Habitat: Eco-justice and the Church's Response*. Edited by Dieter Hessel and Larry Rasmussen. Minneapolis: Fortress, 2001.

Conservation Burial Alliance. Accessed December 4, 2021. https://www.conservationburialalliance.org.

Cook, Justin. "A Cemetery Angel and the American HIV/AIDS Crisis." Collective for Radical Death Studies, August 25, 2019. https://radicaldeathstudies.com/2019/08/25/a-cemetery-angel-and-the-american-hiv-aids-crisis/.

Corrigan, Maureen. "'Let the People See': It Took Courage to Keep Emmett Till's Memory Alive." NPR, October 30, 2018. https://www.npr.org/2018/10/30/660980178/-let-the-people-see-shows-how-emmett-till-s-murder-was-nearly-forgotten.

Cosgrove, Reilly, Sarah Barton, and Devan Stahl. "Disability Theology: A Working Bibliography." *The Faithful OT*. Accessed June 16, 2022. https://thefaithfulot.com/resources/.

Cox, Harvey. *The Market as God*. Cambridge, MA: Harvard University Press, 2016.

Creamer, Deborah Beth. *Disability and Christian Theology: Embodied Limits and Constructive Possibilities*. Oxford: Oxford University Press, 2009.

Cremation Association of North America. "Industry Statistical Information." Accessed December 9, 2021. https://www.cremationassociation.org/page/IndustryStatistics.

Cross, Sarah H., and Haider J. Warraich. "Changes in the Places of Death in the United States." *New England Journal of Medicine*, December 12, 2019. https://www.nejm.org/doi/full/10.1056/NEJMc1911892.

Danby, Herbert, trans. *The Mishnah: Translated from the Hebrew with Introduction and Brief Explanatory Notes*. Oxford: Oxford University Press, 1933.

Davies, Douglas. *Death, Ritual and Belief: The Rhetoric of Funerary Rites*. 3rd ed. London: Bloomsbury, 2017.

Davies, Douglas, and Hannah Rumble. *Natural Burial: Traditional-Secular Spiritualities and Funeral Innovation*. New York: Continuum, 2012.

Davies, W. D. *The Gospel and the Land: Early Christianity and Jewish Territorial Doctrine*. Berkeley: University of California Press, 1974.

Davis, Ellen F. *Scripture, Culture, and Agriculture: An Agrarian Reading of the Bible*. Cambridge: Cambridge University Press, 2008.

DeLand, Lauren. "Live Fast, Die Young, Leave a Useful Corpse: The Terrible Utility of David Wojnarowicz." *Performance Research* 19, no. 1 (2014): 33–40.

Diogenes Laertius. *Lives of Eminent Philosophers*. Vol. 2, bks. 6–10. Translated by R. D. Hicks. LCL 185. Cambridge, MA: Harvard University Press, 1925.

Doughty, Caitlin. *From Here to Eternity: Traveling the World to Find the Good Death*. New York: Norton, 2017.

———. Order of the Good Death. Accessed December 10, 2021. https://www.orderofthegooddeath.com.

———. *Smoke Gets in Your Eyes: And Other Lessons from the Crematory*. New York: Norton, 2014.

Dowdy, Shannon Lee. *American Afterlife: Reinventing Death in the 21st Century*. Princeton, NJ: Princeton University Press, 2021.

Eiesland, Nancy L. *The Disabled God: Toward a Liberatory Theology of Disability*. Nashville: Abingdon, 1994.

Ekerwald, Hedvig. "Me and My Dead Body: Death, Secularism, and Simultaneity." Pages 151–174 in *Death Matters: Cultural Sociology of Mortal Life*. Edited by Tora Holmberg, Annika Jonsson, and Fredrik Palm. Cham, Switzerland: Palgrave Macmillan, 2019.

Everly, Mark. "When Someone Dies, What Happens to the Body?" Conversation, September 15, 2020. https://theconversation.com/when-someone-dies-what-happens-to-the-body-143070.

Faust, Drew Gilpin. *This Republic of Suffering: Death and the Civil War*. New York: Vintage Books, 2008.

Federal Trade Commission Consumer Information. "The FTC Funeral Rule." July 2012. https://www.consumer.ftc.gov/articles/0300-ftc-funeral-rule.

Fletcher, Kami. "Founding Baltimore's Mount Auburn Cemetery and Its Importance to Understanding African American Burial Rights." Pages 129–156 in *Till Death Do Us Part: American Ethnic Cemeteries as Borders Uncrossed*. Edited by Allan Amanik and Kami Fletcher. Jackson: University Press of Mississippi, 2020.

Fournier, Elizabeth. *The Green Burial Guidebook: Everything You Need to Plan an Affordable, Environmentally Friendly Burial*. Novato, CA: New World Library, 2018.

Friends of Mount Auburn. "African American Heritage Trail." Mount Auburn Cemetery, February 1, 2013. https://mountauburn.org/african-american-trail/.

Gabel, Laurel K. "Death, Burial, and Memorialization in Colonial New England: The Diary of Samuel Sewall." *Markers* 25 (2008): 8–43.

Gallagher, Delia, Daniel Burke, and James Masters. "Vatican Issues Guidelines on Cremation, Says No to Scattering Ashes." CNN World, October 25, 2016. https://www.cnn.com/2016/10/25/europe/cremation-vatican-scattering/index.html.

Gay Men's Health Crisis. "History." Accessed November 20, 2021. https://www.gmhc.org/history/.

Gilson, Thomas E., and William Gilson. *Carved in Stone: The Artistry of Early New England Gravestones*. Middletown, CT: Wesleyan University Press, 2012.

Golden, Hallie. "'Give Back to the Earth': Washington Could Legalize Composting of Human Remains." *Guardian*, March 12, 2019. https://www.theguardian.com/us-news/2019/mar/11/human-composting-after-death-washington?CMP=share_btn_link.

Grace Church Natural Burial. "Frequently Asked Questions." Accessed December 6, 2021. https://gracechurchsc.org/naturalburial/faq/.

———. "Natural Burial." Accessed December 4, 2021. https://gracechurchsc.org/naturalburial/.

———. "Why Natural Burial." Accessed December 4, 2021. https://gracechurchsc.org/naturalburial/why/.

Green Burial Council. "Disposition Statistics." Accessed June 19, 2021. https://www.greenburialcouncil.org/media_packet.html.

———. "Green Burial Council Cemetery Certification Standards." December 18, 2019. https://www.greenburialcouncil.org/our_standards.html.

Griffiths, Paul J. *Christian Flesh*. Stanford, CA: Stanford University Press, 2018.

Hanson, Eric, Daniel P. Games, and Alexa Manuel. "The Residential School System." Indigenous Studies UBC. Accessed September 2020. https://indigenousfoundations.arts.ubc.ca/the_residential_school_system/#what-were-residential-schools.

Haraway, Donna J. *Staying with the Trouble: Making Kin in the Chthulucene*. Durham, NC: Duke University Press, 2016.

Harjo, Laura. *Spiral to the Stars: Mvskoke Tools of Futurity*. Tucson: University of Arizona Press, 2019.

Harris, Mark. *Grave Matters: A Journey through the Modern Funeral Industry to a Natural Way of Burial*. New York: Scribner, 2007.

Harris, Melanie L. *Ecowomanism: African American Women and Earth-Honoring Faiths*. Maryknoll, NY: Orbis Books, 2017.

Harrison, Beverly Wildung. "The Power of Anger in the Work of Love: Christian Ethics for Women and Other Strangers." *USQR* 36 (1981): 41–57.

Harrison, Robert Pogue. *The Dominion of the Dead.* Chicago: University of Chicago Press, 2003.

Hegel, G. W. F. *The Philosophy of History*. Translated by J. H. Clarke. New York: Dover, 1956.

Heidegger, Martin. *The Question Concerning Technology*. Translated by William Lovitt. New York: Harper & Row, 1977.

Heritage Acres Memorial Sanctuary. "Home." Accessed December 4, 2021. https://www.heritageacresmemorial.org.

———. "Pricing List." Accessed December. 6, 2021. https://www.heritageacresmemorial.org/pricing-2/.

Herodotus. *Histories.* Vol. 2, bks. 3–4. Translated by A. D. Godley. LCL 118. Cambridge, MA: Harvard University Press, 1921.

Holloway, Karla F. C. *Passed On: African American Mourning Stories*. Durham, NC: Duke University Press, 2003.

Holmberg, Tora, Annika Jonsson, and Fredrik Palm. "Introduction: Why Death Matters." Pages 1–22 in *Death Matters: Cultural Sociology of Mortal Life*. Edited by Tora Holmberg, Annika Jonsson, and Fredrik Palm. Cham, Switzerland: Palgrave Macmillan, 2019.

Holmes, Barbara A. *Crisis Contemplation: Healing the Wounded Village.* Albuquerque, NM: CAC, 2021.

Homer. *Iliad*, Vol. 2, bks. 13–24. Translated by A. T. Murray. Revised by William F. Wyatt. LCL 171. Cambridge, MA: Harvard University Press, 1925.

Honey Creek Woodlands. "Buying a Plot/Pricing." Accessed December 6, 2021. https://www.honeycreekwoodlands.com/buying-a-plot-1.

———. "Home." Accessed December 4, 2021. https://www.honeycreekwoodlands.com.

Hope, Valerie. *Roman Death: The Dying and the Dead in Ancient Rome*. New York: Continuum, 2009.

Horrell, David G., Cherryl Hunt, and Christopher Southgate. *Greening Paul: Rereading the Apostle in a Time of Ecological Crisis*. Waco, TX: Baylor University Press, 2010.

Intergovernmental Panel on Climate Change. "Summary for Policymakers of IPCC Special Report on Global Warming of 1.5°C Approved by Governments." January 21, 2020. https://www.ipcc.ch/2018/10/08/summary-for-policymakers-of-ipcc-special-report-on-global-warming-of-1-5c-approved-by-governments//.

Intergovernmental Science-Policy Platform on Biodiversity and Ecosystem Services. "Media Release: Nature's Dangerous Decline 'Unprecedented'; Species Extinction Rates 'Accelerating.'" Accessed June 23, 2021. https://www.ipbes.net/news/Media-Release-Global-Assessment.

John Paul II. *Theology of the Body: Human Love in the Divine Plan*. New York: Pauline Books and Media, 1997.

Johnson, Luke Timothy. *The Revelatory Body: Theology as Inductive Art*. Grand Rapids, MI: Eerdmans, 2015.

Jones, Diane. "The City of the Dead: The Place of Cultural Identity and Environmental Sustainability in the African-American Cemetery." *Landscape Journal* 30 (2011): 226–240.

Jung, Carl. *Man and His Symbols*. London: Aldus Books, 1964.

Kantor, Jodi. "'We're Going to See What Else the Word Funeral Can Mean." *New York Times*, April 5, 2020. https://www.nytimes.com/2020/04/05/us/coronavirus-dilemmas-mourning.html.

Kaufman, Gordon D. *An Essay on Theological Method*. 3rd ed. Atlanta: Scholars Press, 1995.

———. *The Problem of God*. Cambridge, MA: Harvard University Press, 1972.

Keefe Funeral Home. "Home Vigil Support." Accessed December 10, 2021. https://www.keefefuneralhome.com/home-vigil-support.

Keener, Craig S. *Acts: An Exegetical Commentary*. 4 vol. Grand Rapids, MI: Baker Academic, 2012–2015.

Keijzer, E. E., and H. J. G. Kok. *Environmental Impact of Different Funeral Technologies*. Utrecht: TNO, 2011.

Kelly, Suzanne. *Greening Death: Reclaiming Burial Practices and Restoring Our Tie to the Earth*. New York: Rowman & Littlefield, 2015.

Kloppenborg, John. *Christ's Associations: Connecting and Belonging in the Ancient City*. New Haven, CT: Yale University Press, 2019.

Kolbert, Elizabeth. *The Sixth Extinction: An Unnatural History*. New York: Henry Holt, 2014.

Kraeling, Carl H. "Was Jesus Accused of Necromancy?" *JBL* 59, no. 2 (1940): 147–157.

Krzywoszynska, Anna, and Greta Marchesi. "Toward a Relational Materiality of Soils." *Environmental Humanities* 12, no. 1 (2020): 190–204.

Kuykendall, Ronald. "Hegel and Africa: An Evaluation of the Treatment of Africa in the Philosophy of History." *Journal of Black Studies* 23, no. 4 (1993): 571–581.

Laderman, Gary. *Rest in Peace: A Cultural History of Death and the Funeral Home in Twentieth-Century America*. New York: Oxford University Press, 2003.

———. *The Sacred Remains: American Attitudes toward Death, 1799–1883*. New Haven, CT: Yale University Press, 1996.

Laqueur, Thomas. *The Work of the Dead: A Cultural History of Mortal Remains*. Princeton, NJ: Princeton University Press, 2018.

Latour, Bruno. *Facing Gaia: Eight Lectures on the New Climatic Regime*. Translated by Catherine Porter. Medford, MA: Polity, 2017.

Lederberg, Joshua, and Alexa T. McCray. "'Ome Sweet 'Omics—a Genealogical Treasury of Words." *Scientist* 15, no. 7 (2001): 8.

Levine, A.-J. "Tabitha / Dorcas, Spinning Off Cultural Criticism." Pages 41–65 in *Delightful Acts: New Essays on Canonical and Non-canonical Acts*. Edited by Harold W. Attridge, Dennis R. MacDonald, and Clare K. Rothschild. WUNT 391. Tübingen: Mohr Siebeck, 2017.

Lightfoot, J. L. *Parthenius of Nicaea*. Oxford: Clarendon Press, 1999.

Lincoln Heritage Funeral Advantage. "The Cremation Process from Start to Finish." Accessed June 9, 2021. https://www.lhlic.com/consumer-resources/how-does-cremation-work/#long.

Linden, Blanche M. G. *Silent City on a Hill: Picturesque Landscapes of Memory and Boston's Mount Auburn Cemetery*. Amherst: University of Massachusetts Press, 2007.

Long, Thomas G. *Accompany Them with Singing: The Christian Funeral.* Louisville: Westminster John Knox, 2009.

Long, Thomas G., and Thomas Lynch. *The Good Funeral: Death, Grief, and the Community of Care*. Louisville: Westminster John Knox, 2013.

Lorimer, Jamie. "Rot." *Environmental Humanities* 8, no. 2 (2016): 235–239.

Lucian. *Anacharsis or Athletics. Menippus or The Descent into Hades. On Funerals. A Professor of Public Speaking. Alexander the False Prophet. Essays in Portraiture. Essays in Portraiture Defended. The Goddesse of Surrye*. Translated by A. M. Harmon. LCL 162. Cambridge, MA: Harvard University Press, 1925.

Ludwig, Allan I. *Graven Images: New England Stonecarving and Its Symbols 1650–1815*. Middletown, CT: Wesleyan University Press, 1966.

Magness, Jodi. "Ossuaries and the Burials of Jesus and James." *JBL* 124, no. 1 (2005): 121–154.

Mahoney, Karen. "Bishops Oppose 'Flameless Cremation' Bill." *Catholic Herald*, May 17, 2021. https://catholicherald.org/local/bishops-oppose-flameless-cremation-bill/.

Marsden-Ille, Sara. "What Is the Average Cost of a Cremation?" US Funerals Online, November 26, 2020. https://www.us-funerals.com/what-is-the-average-cost-of-a-cremation/#.YMDK-i-cbdc.

Mayo Clinic. "Body Donation at Mayo Clinic." Accessed December 10, 2021. https://www.mayoclinic.org/body-donation/making-donation.

Mbembe, Achille. *Critique of Black Reason*. Translated by Laurent Dubois. Durham, NC: Duke University Press, 2017.

———. *Necropolitics*. Durham, NC: Duke University Press, 2019.

McDuff, Mallory. *Our Last Best Act: Planning for the End of Our Lives to Protect the People and Places We Love*. Minneapolis: Broadleaf Books, 2021.

McFague, Sally. *The Body of God: An Ecological Theology*. Minneapolis: Fortress, 1993.

Memorial Ecosystems. "Ramsey Creek Preserve History." Accessed December 6, 2021. https://www.memorialecosystems.com/ramsey_creek_preserve_history.html.

Moulaison, Jane Barter. "'Our Bodies, Our Selves?' The Body as Source in Feminist Theology." *SJT* 60 (2007): 341–359.

Mount Auburn Cemetery. "Hymn Sung at Consecration." Accessed August 1, 2014. https://mountauburn.org/hymn-sung-at-consecration/.

National End-of-Life Doula Alliance. "Doulas and After Death Care." Accessed May 13, 2022. https://www.nedalliance.org/after_death_care.html.

National Funeral Directors Association. "Certified Celebrant Training." Accessed June 19, 2021. https://nfda.org/education/certification-training-programs/about-certified-celebrant-training.

———. "Statistics." Accessed June 30, 2020. https://www.nfda.org/news/statistics.

National Home Funeral Alliance. "Home." Accessed December 6, 2021. https://www.homefuneralalliance.org.

Native Hope. "Missing and Murdered Indigenous Women." Accessed November 15, 2021. https://www.nativehope.org/en-us/understanding-the-issue-of-missing-and-murdered-indigenous-women.

Northcote, James Spencer, William R-Brownlow, and Giovanni Battista De Rossi. *Roma Sotterranea: Or, Some Account of the Roman Catacombs.* London: Longman, Green, Reader and Dyer, 1869.

Nouwen, Henri J. M. *A Spirituality of Fundraising.* Nashville: Upper Room Books, 2010.

Ogden, Daniel. *Magic, Witchcraft, and Ghosts in the Greek and Roman Worlds: A Sourcebook.* Oxford: Oxford University Press, 2009.

Osmer, Richard R. *Practical Theology: An Introduction.* Grand Rapids, MI: Eerdmans, 2008.

Outka, Elizabeth. "'Wood for the Coffins Ran Out': Modernism and the Shadowed Afterlife of the Influenza Pandemic." *Modernism/Modernity* 21, no. 4 (2015): 937–960.

Palliative Care, Stanford School of Medicine. "Where Do Americans Die?" Accessed June 9, 2021. https://palliative.stanford.edu/home-hospice-home-care-of-the-dying-patient/where-do-americans-die/.

Pennsylvania Historical and Museum Commission. "1900–Present: Lawn-Park Cemeteries and Memorial Parks." August 26, 2015. http://www.phmc.state.pa.us/portal/communities/cemetery-preservation/development/1900-present.html.

Peterson, Jane, Susan Garges, Maria Givanni, Pamela McInnes, Lu Wang, Jeffrey A. Schloss, Vivien Bonazzi, et al. "The NIH Human Microbiome Project." *Genome Research* 19, no. 12 (2009): 2317–2323. https://www.ncbi.nlm.nih.gov/pmc/articles/PMC2792171/#B13.

Pine Hill Cemetery Association. "Grave Liner and Vault Options." Accessed June 9, 2021. http://pinehillcemeterydavenport.com/media//DIR_4401/7b2aa0364051e060ffff804effffe904.pdf.

Prothero, Stephen. *Purified by Fire: A History of Cremation in America.* Berkeley: University of California Press, 2001.

Queer Death Studies Network. "About." Accessed November 13, 2021. https://queerdeathstudies.net.

Rankine, Claudia. "The Condition of Black Life Is One of Mourning." Pages 145–155 in *The Fire This Time: A New Generation Speaks about Race.* Edited by Jesmyn Ward. New York: Scribner, 2016.

Rebillard, Éric. "Violation of Tombs and Impiety: Funerary Practices and Religious Beliefs." Pages 57–88 in *The Care of the Dead in Late Antiquity.* Translated by Elizabeth Trapnell Rawlings and Jeanine Routier-Pucci. Cornell Studies in Classical Philology 59. Ithaca, NY: Cornell University Press, 2009.

Recompose. "Environmental Impact." Accessed December 10, 2021. https://recompose.life/our-model/#the-forest.

———. "Recompose." Accessed December 10, 2021. https://recompose.life.

Rothstein, Karla, and Christina Staudt. "Introduction." Pages xv–xxi in *The Future of the Corpse: Changing Ecologies of Death and Disposition.* Edited by Karla Rothstein and Christina Staudt. Santa Barbara, CA: Praeger, 2021.

Sachs, Aaron. *Arcadian America: The Death and Life of an Environmental Tradition.* New Haven, CT: Yale University Press, 2013.

Safrai, Shemuel. "Home and Family." Pages 2:728–792 in *The Jewish People in the First Century.* 2 Volumes. Edited by S. Safrai and M. Stern in cooperation with D. Flusser and W. C. van Unnik. Amsterdam: Van Gorcum, 1974, 1976.

Samuels, Elyse, and Adriana Usero. "'New York City's Family Tomb': The Sad History of Hart Island." *Washington Post,* April 27, 2020. https://www.washingtonpost.com/history/2020/04/27/hart-island-mass-grave-coronavirus-burials/.

Sanders, Cody J. "Decentering the Human in Practical Theologies of Care: An EARTH Method." *International Journal of Practical Theology,* in press.

———. "How the Covid-19 Pandemic May Permanently Change Our 'Good Death' Narrative." *Religion Dispatches,* April 2, 2020. https://religiondispatches.org/how-the-covid-19-pandemic-may-permanently-change-our-good-death-narrative/.

———. "Mor(t)al Remains: Pastoral Theology and Corpse Care." *Journal of Pastoral Theology* 29, no. 2 (2019): 116–131.

Schoenwetter, Christina. "When We Can't Gather, How Do We Mourn?" *Sojourners,* June 9, 2020. https://sojo.net/articles/when-we-cant-gather-how-do-we-mourn.

Searle, Adam. "Absence." *Environmental Humanities* 12, no. 1 (2020): 167–172.

Seeman, Erik R. *Death in the New World: Cross-Cultural Encounters, 1492–1800.* Philadelphia: University of Pennsylvania Press, 2010.

Service Corporation International. "Investor Fact Sheet." Accessed June 19, 2021. https://filecache.investorroom.com/mr5ir_scicorp/194/Investor-Fact-Sheet%202020%20Q4%20FINAL.pdf.

———. "Investor Overview." Accessed June 19, 2021. https://investors.sci-corp.com.

Sharpe, Christina. *In the Wake: On Blackness and Being.* Durham, NC: Duke University Press, 2016.

Sheldrake, Merlin. *Entangled Life: How Fungi Make Our Worlds, Change Our Minds, and Shape Our Futures.* New York: Random House, 2020.

Shotwell, Alexis. *Against Purity: Living Ethically in Compromised Times.* Minneapolis: University of Minnesota Press, 2016.

Sloane, David Charles. "Nature versus Culture: Shifting Values in American Cemeteries." Pages 119–142 in *The Future of the Corpse: Changing Ecologies of Death and Disposition.* Edited by Karla Rothstein and Christina Staudt. Santa Barbara, CA: Praeger, 2021.

Slocum, Joshua, and Lisa Carlson. *Final Rights: Reclaiming the American Way of Death.* Hinesburg, VT: Upper Access Books, 2011.

Smith, Jeffrey E. "Till Death Keeps Us Apart: Segregated Cemeteries and Social Values in St. Louis, Missouri." Pages 157–181 in *Till Death Do Us Part: American Ethnic Cemeteries as Borders Uncrossed.* Edited by Allan Amanik and Kami Fletcher. Jackson: University Press of Mississippi, 2020.

Stannard, David E. *The Puritan Way of Death: A Study in Religion, Culture, and Social Change.* New York: Oxford University Press, 1977.

Stevens, Holly, and Donna Belk. *Undertaken with Love: A Home Funeral Guide for Families and Community Care Groups*. Everett, WA: National Home Funeral Alliance, 2016.

Stewart, Benjamin M. "Committed to the Earth: Ecotheological Dimensions of Christian Burial Practices." *Liturgy* 27, no. 2 (2012): 62–72.

———. "The Place of the Earth in Lutheran Funeral Rites: Mapping the Current Terrain." *Dialogue: A Journal of Theology* 52, no. 2 (2014): 118–126.

Story, Joseph. "An Address Delivered on the Dedication of the Cemetery at Mount Auburn, September 24, 1831." Mount Auburn Cemetery, September 24, 2011. https://mountauburn.org/joseph-storys-consecration-address/.

Stroud, Ellen. "Law and the Dead Body: Is a Corpse a Person or a Thing?" *Annual Review of Law and Social Science* 14 (2018): 115–125.

Tashjian, Dickran, and Ann Tashjian. *Memorials for Children of Change: The Art of Early New England Stonecarving*. Middletown, CT: Wesleyan University Press, 1974.

Toynbee, J. M. C. *Death and Burial in the Roman World*. Ithaca, NY: Cornell University Press, 1971.

Troyer, John Erik. "Technologies of the HIV/AIDS Corpse." *Medical Anthropology* 29, no. 2 (2010): 129–149.

Walker-Barnes, Chanequa. "Response to Rev. Michael McBride Plenary, 'Conversions in the Age of Trump' Society for Pastoral Theology, June 14, 2018." *Journal of Pastoral Theology* 29, no. 1 (2019): 13–18.

Wallace, Mark I. *When God Was a Bird: Christianity, Animism, and the Re-enchantment of the World*. New York: Fordham University Press, 2019.

Warren, Karen J. "The Power and Promise of Ecological Feminism." *Environmental Ethics* 12 (1990): 125–146.

Weber, Andreas. *Enlivenment: Toward a Poetics for the Anthropocene*. Cambridge, MA: MIT Press, 2019.

Webster, Lee., ed. *Changing Landscapes: Exploring the Growth of Ethical, Compassionate, and Environmentally Sustainable Green Funeral Service*. Self-published, CreateSpace, 2016.

Webster, Lee. "Home Funerals and Green Burial." Lecture. Andover Newton Theological School, Newton, MA, April 17, 2018.

———. "Rethinking the Role of the Funeral Director." Pages 143–177 in *The Future of the Corpse: Changing Ecologies of Death and Disposition*. Edited by Karla Rothstein and Christina Staudt. Santa Barbara, CA: Praeger, 2021.

Webster, Lee, Carl Anderson, Kristen Bass, John Meagher, Lindsay Soyer, Merilynne Rush, and Steven Whitman. "The Science behind Green and Conventional Burial." Green Burial Council. Accessed November 30, 2021. https://www.greenburialcouncil.org/uploads/1/2/4/2/124231485/the_science_behind_green_burial.pdf.

Webster, Lee, and Donna Belk. *Planning Guide and Workbook for Home Funeral Families*. Everett, WA: National Home Funeral Alliance, 2015.

West, Nancy. "Pictures of Death." *Atlantic*, July 19, 2017. https://www.theatlantic.com/technology/archive/2017/07/pictures-of-death/534060/.

Winsor, Morgan, and Emily Shapiro. "US Coronavirus Death Toll Surpasses 60,000 and 100 Bodies Found in Trucks Outside NYC Funeral Home." ABC

News, April 30, 2020. https://abcnews.go.com/Health/coronavirus-updates-us-federal-inmate-dies-covid-19/story?id=70399771.

Wirzba, Norman. *This Sacred Life: Humanity's Place in a Wounded World.* New York: Cambridge University Press, 2021.

World Wildlife Fund. "Soil Erosion and Degradation: Overview." Accessed March 31, 2019. https://www.worldwildlife.org/threats/soil-erosion-and-degradation.

Wright, N. T. *The Resurrection of the Son of God.* Minneapolis: Fortress, 2003.

Wright, Roberta Hughes, and Wilbur B. Hughes III. *Lay Down Body: Living History in African American Cemeteries.* Detroit: Visible Ink, 1996.

Young, Ed. *I Contain Multitudes: The Microbes within Us and a Grander View of Life.* New York: Ecco, 2016.

Index